Jehovah Jireh

Pearl Coleman

New Wine Press

New Wine Press
PO Box 17
Chichester
West Sussex PO20 6YB
England

All Bible quotations are from the Authorised Version.

ISBN: 1 874367 36 1

Typeset by CRB Associates, Norwich.
Printed in England by Clays Ltd, St Ives plc.

Dedication

This book is dedicated to my secretary Ruth Daniels, the attack on whom was so great when she was typing the manuscript. In spite of severe and unremitting pain she was dedicated to the task, mindful of the spiritual warfare we were all in, and how much the devil wanted to prevent the Asian population, in particular, becoming informed and consequently set free. Without Ruth's endurance and faithfulness and, above all, trust in her Jehovah Jireh there would have been no manuscript and no book, for she encouraged me while in the fury of the battle. We linked our shields of faith together and warded off all the fiery darts of the wicked.

'Now thanks be unto God, which always causeth us to triumph in Christ, and maketh manifest the savour of his knowledge by us in every place.'
(2 Corinthians 2:14)

'But thanks be to God, which giveth us the victory through our Lord Jesus Christ. Therefore, my beloved brethren, be ye stedfast, unmoveable, always abounding in the work of the Lord, forasmuch as ye know that your labour is not in vain in the Lord.'
(1 Corinthians 15:57–8)

Pearl Coleman

Contents

Acknowledgements

My love and thanks and heartfelt gratitude goes to those who were moved by His Spirit to pray for me, to fund my trips to the East and to help with the constant expenses of providing a Clinic and Sanctuary which glorifies the Lord. He saw your giving and heard your prayers. He knows your names. May you be always blessed and know His provision in every area of your lives.

> *'Give, and it shall be given unto you; good measure, pressed down, and shaken together, and running over, shall men give into your bosom. For with the same measure that ye mete withal it shall be measured to you again.'* (Luke 7:38)

> *'Cast thy bread upon the waters: for thou shalt find it after many days.'* (Ecclesiasticus 11:1)

> *'For the Scripture saith, Thou shalt not muzzle the ox that treadeth out the corn. And, the labourer is worthy of his reward.'* (1 Timothy 5:18)

Chapter 1

The Names of The Lord

Our Lord has so many names. May they all be honoured and known to His people, for it is written:

> *'And it shall come to pass, that whosoever shall call upon the name of the Lord shall be saved.'*
>
> (Acts 2:21)

I praise the Lord that I have known Him, and indeed at some time or another called upon Him by each of His names. Those names and their meaning are listed below, as they are such a blessing to learn:

Jehovah Tsidkenu – The Lord God our Righteousness
Jehovah M'kaddesh – The Lord God my Sanctification
Jehovah Shalom – The Lord God is Peace
Jehovah Shammah – The Lord God at hand
Jehovah Rophi – The Lord God my Healer
Jehovah Rohi – The Lord God my Shepherd
Jehovah Nissi – The Lord God my Bannner
Jehovah Jireh – The Lord God will provide

Yes, I have known the blessing of His every name. He has healed me as Jehovah Rophi, sanctified me as Jehovah M'kaddesh, been close to me in times of trouble as Jehovah Shammah.

He has led me into victory against the evil one as Jehovah Nissi, and gathered me again into His fold as Jehovah Rohi when I have strayed like a lost sheep (Psalm 23).

He has been my Jehovah Shalom, the Lord my Peace in times of trouble and unbelievable turmoil, experienced in this long, long spiritual warfare that threatens, not infrequently, to engulf me. Ever since I learned to hate the Devil and all his works, and to confront him, I have known the impossibility of the battle without His abiding Peace. How I Praise Him for that Peace.

He has been Jehovah Tsidkenu, the Lord my Righteousness, as I have hungered and thirsted, and indeed do hunger and thirst, after Him, that I might be continually filled with His Spirit. But most of all I have known Him intimately as Jehovah Jireh, the Lord my Provider, and seen Him in this capacity for so many broken and wretched people, who have arived at the Clinic often at the end of a desperate life's journey.

I fall down on my knees and worship Him, in wonder and amazement at His extravagant love, His mercy and grace for me, who has been in so many ways a wayward child, falling far short of what He requires in terms of servanthood. That I am committed to Him, I trust nobody will doubt. That I am constantly in the refining crucible must be obvious to those around me, and I have no doubt that I shall still be there when the time comes to meet Him in the air.

How I long for that day. When you pray 'Thy kingdom come', tell me honestly, do you mean it? Do you really mean it? Have you had enough of the deception and abominations of this world? Or would you like to just fit in one more holiday at the Costa Brava, or complete the extension on your house? Be honest now! Have you come out of the world, and does it pale into insignificance when you concentrate on Him?

Being in the crucible is always so painful, but there is always the joy of His strength, the peace of obedience to His calling. The flesh continually wars against the Spirit, I do not deny, but there is no other way for me to contemplate than a life in Christ, and all that it means, including a certain loneliness. It is a life laid down.

I can say in truth that 1993 to May 15th 1994, when I am commencing this, my fourth book, have been months of indescribable battle and pain, the most agonising time of my life. A time when I have challenged Satan in a new way, and experienced his devious, disgusting and cunning schemes to throw me off the path I have resolutely chosen to follow.

'Father, what is going on?' I have cried out so often, in common with many illustrious ones, I note!

The response to my *crie de coeur* always seems to be:

> 'Pour out, pour out, pour out, and be ready to do so even to the last drop of blood.'

Even now as I am commencing this book, I am releasing something so precious to me. I am faced with grievous loss in many areas, and I am crying out to Jehovah Jireh my Provider, for I shall indeed need to know Him as just that in a very big way!

Pondering over the amazing events of this last year and the future set before me, I have cause to reflect upon His amazing provision as a confirmation and a comfort that I am on the right path, although it hurts so much.

Jehovah Jireh is such a reality to me, not an ill-defined, vague person of the Godhead. I see His continual provision for me as a sign of His favour. I do not see it in any other way.

I see that same favour shown by Him to so many drowning souls who reach the Clinic mentally, physically and spiritually at the end of their tether. All of them are Born Again Believers but infirm, confused, drained, numbed by grief.

Some are leaning on the arms of loved ones, or padding about on all fours like dogs, plagued by the curse of bestiality. Some cannot give their history for weeping, or clutch plastic buckets into which they have been vomiting at regular intervals for years. Victims of demonic possession, oppression, medical accident, drug toxicity (iatrogenic – induced inadvertently by prescription – or illicit). Victims of abuse, terror, hatred, poverty, rejection and so on.

There are of course those who are reaping the harvest of their own indulgences or self-abuse one way or the other, but this is not as common as the other destructions.

I frequently say we would not be in business if the Church was not sick. Astonishingly, only about one percent of those who arrive here now are unsaved, and of course they don't get away (unsaved)! It is very clear to me that the Clinic is God's provision for His people, part of the End Time preparation of His bride by the Holy Spirit for Jesus' approaching return, and He gets them here in a very unique way each time.

In praise, honour and glory to His holy name, at this time of raging battle, I have been caused to reflect upon how I first came to know Him as Jehovah Jireh my Provider. It's like He is saying as I write:

'You get it down and you will find that I am still your provision.'

I shall relate the blessings of others to whom He has been Jehovah Jireh, but I'll begin with myself.

Chapter 2

Forsaken

It was a crisp early autumn morning. My doctor had been sketching my bruises onto a simple diagram of my anatomy. I spent a short time at the local X-Ray unit and made my way home. In all I was absent about two hours. I needed a hot drink.

Parking my car in the long drive I sauntered round to the front door, inserting my key in the lock. Pushing the pine door open I stepped inside.

'That's funny,' I thought, as my shoes made a noisy sound beneath me. I was used to the crunchy greeting of cosy carpet tiles as I would kick off my outdoor shoes and grab my slippers from the shoe box at the entrance, placing my handbag on the dresser.

There was just a lonely telephone sitting upon the entrance hall window sill, with a few telephone directories, to greet me. No dresser? I gazed in disbelief at the formerly carpeted quarry tiles.

As I pushed open the glazed door which separated the entrance hall from the middle hall I was aware of a hollow ringing sound. It was the radiators echoing as the boiler came on to high flame, as I had let the cool air into the house. I recalled they did this when we first viewed the house for sale some twenty years previously in winter time, when the building was empty but the central heating left on for potential buyers.

I went into shock, trembling as I walked from room to room. The home had been stripped of so many friendly pieces of furniture. I raced to the bedroom. I needed to lay down. There was no bed!

I tottered into the kitchen to put on the kettle for that life-saving cup of tea. No kettle! No kitchen table! It had been an eight-seater pine table. The kitchen looked so bare. Each room brought further shock as I opened the door.

I would go upstairs to my consulting room, it was bound to be alright. Alas, the huge Indian carpet had been removed to reveal a large rectangle of unpolished floorboards. The pine desk was no more. In those days I used to see patients in the evenings. What should I do? So great was my fear and trembling that when the patients did arive at 7.00 pm I had forgotten all about them! They were extremely understanding and released me from the obligation of the consultation.

I wasn't too worried about sleeping on the floor because I knew I had a spare duvet and sheets in the airing cupboard. My joy was short-lived when I found that these also had gone.

So there I was, in my formerly comfortable home, devoid of many treasures and comforts I had long taken for granted. One accumulates a lot of things in twenty-three years of marriage, and I thank God that the Lord showed me during the next few years how totally unimportant they all were, every single one of them!

I praise God that I was able to make a fresh start, purchasing only that which would glorify His Clinic. All the occult carvings and pieces of questionable purity had been removed, praise the Lord. His Clinic and Sanctuary

16

it surely became, as readers of my three books, *Go and Do Likewise*, *Fruit Abiding in the Vine* and *The Anointing Breaks the Yoke*, will know.

What an awful journey it has been in pursuit of holiness, but on that autumn morning of shock and disbelief I did not know my Father as I know Him now. The days rolled by as I learned my new role as a deserted wife, bringing one horrific revelation after another.

The mortgage had not been paid for some time. The general rates were in deficit by several hundred pounds, and Lord Denning had just ruled that wives remaining in jointly owned properties now had to pay for them! The gutters fell off in a storm, there was a fault in the central heating which could not be sorted out easily, and for some peculiar reason the water pressure for the hose and kitchen tap became pathetically low.

But this last problem became a lesser concern as I wrestled with the debts, visions of my being expelled from the house filling my mind as I learned to sleep on the hard floor and plan how to purchase essentials like a bed, carpet for the consulting room and kitchen table, etc.

I was still working as a journalist and retained two columns of my own in a couple of magazines, but this was chicken-feed. My patients were always charged very little because I felt I did not really need the money when I started off. I just loved the work God had given me to do.

About ten days after the shock of the removal of a large proportion of the contents of the home, I sat under the loggia on an old garden seat, looking up into the golden foliage of the giant oaks which bordered the lane. I was very tired and also very thin, having lost a lot of weight. Summer was ending, the leaves beginning to fall.

The trouble was that all the paper work on the property; mortgage, rates, insurances really frightened me. Phone bills, gas, electricity, water rates, I wasn't accustomed to handling all these. I didn't know how to do it. The income tax was a nightmare. I had been a director in my former husband's company, which had to be closed down, but he had always looked after the income tax. Why should I pay for water anyway, when it was hardly coming out of the tap? I couldn't even shower properly. So many worries all at once.

The giant oaks loomed majestically against a darkening sky. It was growing chilly. What should I do? I must go in soon or I would catch a cold. I sat there, slightly stiff by now. I should shut the French doors.

But I remained where I was, and grew locked in a fear that, as I had lost my husband, and my furniture and possessions, the next thing would be to lose this beautiful old house which had been renovated so skilfully by my former husband's capable hands. He had been the electrician, plumber, carpenter, painter, paperer, etc., all with excellence. I had been the decorator's mate but unless he was there to instruct I would be useless.

Gardening was fine. I was always the gardener but high hedges and electric hedge-cutters were beyond me. The old hand-push mower was not easy to use either, I discovered! I was fighting off arthritis in my hands.

I was attending the Anglican Church at the time. I'd been going since I was three, but only in my forties did I encounter the Holy Spirit. My eyes were still riveted on the sky and the trees as I called out,

'Oh, Father, what shall I do?'

The reply came very swiftly, 'Tithe.'

'Tithe?' I questioned, 'With what?'

'Make me an offer,' came the response.

'£2 a week,' I said, roughly calculating that I might just notch up an income of £8 per week!

To my shame I didn't really know much about tithing. I thought it was for rich people. Also I tithed my time to the sick. I thought that made it alright. Anyway, I set up a tithe of £8 a month and simply wrote the cheque out as each new month dawned.

Chapter 3

The Water Board Cometh!

I could not use the hose or the shower with effect. In those days I had no washing machine so that did not matter. I believe I was the last woman in town to have one!

I telephoned the water authority and they came at once.

'That's good', I thought.

I told them where I thought the stop-cock was and they went off to investigate the leafy borders of the property. They were simply ages finding it and I left them to it. About an hour later my front door bell rang. Mr Waterboard was standing there with about three feet of totally rusted-through water pipe.

'There's your problem, Madam,' he said somewhat gleefully. 'You were about to have a mains supply pipe burst and it is extremely urgent for it to be done, as the property next door and your own will definitely be flooded if it goes, and it can do literally any day.'

'Praise God,' I exclaimed. 'When will you start?'

The official looked surprised as he informed me

'No, Madam, we've done our bit from the stopcock to the mains pipe. From the house to the stopcock is your responsibility. We'll write to you. You will have to employ a private contractor.'

I stood there absolutely aghast at the news, steadying myself by holding the doorpost.

'How much will it cost?'

'A lot, Madam. There's at least one hundred feet of mains pipe needed, and the digger will have to make a trench about twelve to fifteen feet deep through your shrubbery and across the lawn. Unfortunately we note the supply then disappears under the concrete footage of the greenhouse at the back and then out under your rear courtyard. The labour could easily be £1200, depending upon who you get, but I suggest you have several quotes. I'm sorry we cannot help, but it is very urgent and we have to insist on the work being carried out immediately.'

The official departed. I returned indoors with a splitting headache. Where would this money come from? What would the materials cost? I slumped down in the kitchen on one of the remaining chairs.

'Father,' I cried, 'What shall I do?'

In bed that night as I lay praying, the Holy Spirit indicated a patient of mine, a very, very remarkable and courageous young man called Jonathan. Jonathan was the plumber son of a plumbing family. He came to the Clinic terribly sick with he didn't know what, and ultimately a very serious problem of lead poisoning was revealed following a hair analysis carried out by a medical laboratory. We spent several months chelating the lead out of his system.

I had become aware of the ramifications of lead poisoning as a medical journalist twenty years ago and I saw at first hand the cost and the battle of presenting the truth to the population and governments against such vested interests. I saw many reputable scientists under

22

serious threat and pressures from powerful companies producing lead for petrol, when the awful truth could no longer be disputed that lead in petrol had brain-damaged generations of our children. Finally we got our lead-free petrol, but few know the harassment that was endured by such people as Professor Derek Bryce Smith of Reading University, Department of Chemistry.

It was in contending such unbelievable evils as lead in petrol and fluoridation of public water supplies that I first encountered the sinister deception of the population by so-called authorities and dubious statisticians. As Chairman of the Pure Water Society of Great Britain for some twenty years, with a valiant band of workers we fought off the fluoridation of Surrey water supplies by public debate and counter-attack of its illustrious advocates, and won. Wherever I took the platform and spoke against fluoridation, invariably contesting doctors and dentists who were pro-fluoridation, we always secured an overwhelming majority when the vote was taken.

It's hard to believe now that I had over a million words published on that subject alone! It was all good preparation for the End Times duping of the population by the media, which is undoubtedly going to get worse, praise the Lord! In everything give thanks! I know I'm digressing, but I always do, so readers will be used to that! Back to my own problem of the degenerated mains supply pipe.

A letter arrived within 24 hours stressing the urgency of the replacement. Within that time I had contacted Jonathan as the Lord had led me to. He came over like a shot, bless him, and examined the scene. He agreed it was a nasty job, and said he would carry out all the labour for nothing! The materials were expensive but he saved me about £900 in labour charges – and he was also God's provision for me in another unexpected way.

During the reconnection of the mains supply he had to go into the loft to check the mains tank, which had been installed in 1923. It was literally about to spring a leak and flood the whole loft space over my bedroom. Because of the age of the property with beamed ceilings and asbestos boards, which had to be sealed when the dangers to health from such boards became known, the effects of such a leak could have been a major disaster for me, financially and in terms of stress, of which I had just about had enough.

Not only did Jonathan remove this enormous tank on his back and carry up an even heavier one single-handed and install it on a new platform he built, he further blessed me by not charging me a penny and gave me the tank at cost price! Jonathan was God's provision for me in what could have been a disastrous time of expense. Fourteen years later he is still healthy and active with no recurrence of any of his problems. Paise the Lord, he continues to be extremely well and active.

Chapter 4

The Storm

Shortly after that episode there was a nasty storm which made it imperative to finally dispense with the old fashioned metal guttering in favour of PVC. Water also came in through the ceiling of the patients' toilet and I found several roof tiles smashed on the lawn and courtyard.

At that time I didn't have a patient in the roofing business so I had to consult the directory. I chose three firms. The first gave a cursory inspection and said about a dozen tiles needed replacing and the roof hips needed repointing. He gave me a price.

The second firm took a ladder, following an estimation from below, and agreed with the former quotation. There was little to choose between them. The third firm seemed to be going to such a lot of trouble. I had already spoken to the man on the telephone, saying two firms had quoted me about £199 for the work and there were about twelve tiles to replace plus the pointing. I explained my situation and said any improvement on that figure and the job would be his.

Upon arrival he took from his lorry what I now know to be a cat ladder, the only safe method of inspecting an old roof like that of the Clinic. He very carefully hooked this on the roof centre and climbed up deftly. He examined all four sides of the roof and returned to the back door looking very serious indeed.

'Twelve tiles, Madam,' he said, 'more like sixty, and most are new fractures. Did the previous people examining the roof use a cat ladder? A roof of that age should never be walked upon. The tiles are hard to replace as it is and they are extremely brittle. I would say the recent inspections are the cause of most of the trouble, and to be honest, I think you could make out a case if you know which of the two firms it was.'

Well of course I couldn't, and I felt so cheated, so vulnerable. I was already involved in a lawsuit to keep the property and not have it sold over my head. I was juggling finances and trying to set up a full-time Clinic with all this going on – digging, bulldozing, workmen fixing the central heating and gutters and so on ad nauseam.

I was so tired. I also had to get a decorator in to repair where the fitted furniture had been quickly wrenched off the walls, damaging the plaster and leaving hideous tide marks. Again, a decorator rescued from the grip of arthritis was God's provision for me in that area.

No, I simply could not face legal action or even look for another firm to quote me on the roof. This guy was clearly a professional and not a cowboy! He had taken such care in the inspection that I trusted him. I called out to my Father and He gave me the go ahead, but I had no idea where the money was coming from.

I was scrimping, scraping and half-starving myself to refurnish. I cashed endowment policies and all the small amounts of money I could get my hands on. For something like forty weeks I used the free advertisement in the local paper to advertise items for sale, £10 or under. I emptied the loft of things stored up there for twenty-odd years. My former husband used to say,

'Don't give me anything else to put in the roof or the ceilings will fall in.'

There were tennis racquets, lampshades, old sets of curtains neatly laundered, chairs which needed gluing, bamboo bead curtains, life-jackets and heaven knows what. Every single item sold, and those weeks I would literally live off that £10 for food and petrol. Patients had no idea of the struggle I was having!

The appointed day came for the work on the roof. I recall it was a Thursday Clinic day. The day before the man had assembled building materials in a section of the courtyard I had undertaken to keep clear for him. I grew quite hysterical inside as the materials piled up. Numerous ladders, piles of sand and cement, great stacks of tiles. On the morning of the Clinic I opened the front door to admit Di, one of my staff, gasping as I saw the mound of stuff heaped alongside the wall.

I broke down at prayer time.

'I cannot stand it,' I wept. 'I do not even know what it will cost.'

'Let's pray,' said Di calmly.

She sat next to me on the sofa and led me in a prayer which she called rolling the care on the Lord.

'Cast the care of this bill on Him, Pearl,' she urged me. 'That's what the Bible tells us to do.'

Well, I wasn't very spiritual in those days. I had not studied the Word like I have since, but Di had and I respected her and obeyed.

'I cannot cope with this problem, Lord,' I wailed in self-pity. 'I leave it at the foot of your cross. I cast this burden at your feet, Lord, and I will not take it back, I promise you.'

27

The man was up there all day. The staff left for home at six o'clock and at about seven o'clock came the expected knock at the door. How I was praying as he handed me the bill in a sealed envelope.

'It's OK, post it on,' he said.

I was trusting in God when I replied 'It's alright, I'll get you a cheque whilst you are backing the lorry out.'

'Fine,' he replied.

I opened the envelope, still calling on God in my spirit. I could not believe my eyes. It was the same bill as for twelve tiles and the hips repointing. I hurriedly wrote a cheque, but as I handed it to him my conscience pricked. He had been a very careful, diligent, professional worker. So I said,

'I think there is some mistake. You have only charged me the original quote. You were here all day and there were all those tiles.'

He took the cheque and started up his lorry at the same time. Gazing at me intently, he said,

'Yes, I know. I don't know why I did that.'

'Are you a Christian?' I asked.

'No, I'm certainly not that,' he replied, and sped off up the lane!

So that was Jehovah Jireh, using a man of the world to furnish the need of one of His people, praise His holy name!

Chapter 5

Manna from Heaven

Two years on, with the Clinic beautifully but sparingly furnished, the garden reconstructed with my own hands, including the planting of many new hedgerows which had replaced ancient privet and the digging in of something like thirty trees of about four years maturity, I was very tired but extremely happy casting out demons, enjoying the gift of the discerning of spirits and generally running the enemy off.

I spared nothing of my energy or time to see that the sanctuary glorified the Lord. Always I was budgeting. I raised my tithe as I earned more, but there were no luxuries like holidays or hairdos! If I purchased hand cream for myself one week I had to cut down on milk, although up front it all looked very prosperous.

I learned how to regulate the use of gas and electricity. When it was not a Clinic day the heating went off and the woolies went on! I learned to time outgoing phone calls and to save old envelopes for re-use. Every plastic bag was kept as a bin liner, I grated salads to make them go further and so on.

I lived on sardines, jacket potatoes, omelettes, and a treat was best end of neck of lamb or rolled stuffed breasts. But I was so grateful to God, always praising and thanking Him especially for the Holy Spirit. I spent hours singing to Him as I bustled about, always believing that He would preserve the Clinic for me.

My lawyer was constantly urging me to find someone to give me a mortgage on the present valuation of the house, purchased when the property market was low, now valued at a ridiculous price by a local estate agent. This was hopeless, as I was not only over fifty but I hadn't a record of sufficient earnings and my present salary was fluctuating from week to week. I could not state that I was earning X number of pounds per annum. It was impossible.

I thought that was tough, since I had been the one to pay off the mortgage debt and maintain the property whilst its value increased. The building society I was with simply treated my request for an increased loan with disdain, as did my Bank Manager. In fact, they all thought I should sell up, except my splendid lawyer who was the son of one of my Church elders.

God had given me a very diligent and competent lawyer, a very special man. He seemed to have a real witness of what was going on at the Clinic and was extremely kind and helpful and encouraging. He knew I could not set up a Clinic elsewhere, and he also knew I was diligent and determined to be independent of the State.

Money was tight, ministry was abundant and I soon witnessed that unlike the Asians, the British are not forthcoming on giving! I have also learned in recent years many are ignorant of tithing and say it is Old Testament! Whatever happened I increased my tithe and my giving. I made it a priority and I saw God's blessing, as He promises in Malachi 3:10–11a:

> *'Bring ye all the tithes into the storehouse, that there may be meat in mine house, and prove me now*

*herewith, saith the Lord of Hosts, if I will not open
you the windows of heaven, and pour you out a blessing ... And I will rebuke the devourer for your
sakes, and he shall not destroy the fruits of your
ground.'*

One day, driving to Guildford market in search of
cheaper fruit and vegetables, I saw a roadside notice
advertising very cheap tomatoes and beans. I had seen
this notice often but never investigated where it led.

On this particular morning I pulled up and saw a
small driveway and an arrow saying 'To the Sheds'. I
followed it round and it widened into a yard and a lot of
derelict old farm buildings with shabby corrugated
roofs. There was also a farm house set back off the
road. I pulled up behind an old van and got out. I was
wearing a pale blue pleated skirt and a blue cotton jum-
per. I'll never forget it.

I was greeted by a tall grey-haired man of immense
stature. Later I learned he was in his seventies, but his
brawny arms spoke of a man much younger who had
spent his days lifting crates of heavy vegetables and
sacks of potatoes. His check shirtsleeves were rolled up
to display a few tatoos and I responded to his smile of
welcome with a 'Good morning'.

I told him I had come to investigate what he had to
sell as I had often seen the notices. He seemed to be
staring.

'Well, you are a picture,' he told me quite openly, 'I
don't get many round here like you. Come in, my darling, and see for yourself.'

I thought he had to be Romany. He ushered me into
the inner sanctum of the former cowshed. I gasped.
What a display of fruit and vegetables, farm eggs and
honey met my eyes. It was all half the price of such food

in the supermarkets. I had a field day. I even bought melon and avocado pears. It was cheaper than the cheapest town market.

Well, this became the source of all my purchases of fruit, vegetables, eggs and honey! The man was called Ben.

'Call me Ben,' he invited, 'everybody does.'

He would watch me examining every purchase very closely and I always noticed he gave me much over the weight I ordered, almost double. He was very polite. He would let me select everything, even put it in the scales myself, and he would always throw in something extra to what I weighed.

I felt his eyes on me as I picked out my green groceries. It was not a gaze of lust, but one of deep interest. Then one day he said,

'You're a very careful shopper, aren't you, dear? Very particular.'

'Yes, I've had to be, especially recently, but my mother brought me up that way. We were not allowed to fritter or waste and we always had to look for value.'

'I'd like to meet your mother,' he remarked, and to my surprise I found myself saying,

'I'll introduce you. She is almost eighty, and she is extremely beautiful.'

'Just like her daughter, I shouldn't wonder, beautiful inside and out.'

I took the bull by the horns. I knew this wasn't flattery. I liked the man immensely. We had grown to chat each time I visited the old farm and he shared a lot of his past with me. He had a strong spirit of grief and mourning over his wife who died some years ago.

'Ben, do you know Jesus?' I asked him.

It began like that and led to a long discussion about God, about His creation, His provision of deliverance, and Ben, almost in unbelief, was delivered of grief and mourning over his vegetable stand. He was a dear man, bless him.

There were some weeks I missed going and following one such he asked me,

'Where were you, darling? I was worried. Did you have enough to eat?'

I explained that patient phone calls would sometimes preclude me getting out to shop but I was fine, he was not to worry. I was duly touched by his genuine concern.

'Look, Sunshine,' he said one day, 'if you cannot get to me, ring up and I'll deliver it for you. I can leave it on your doorstep under the porch.'

'Do you do that for anyone else?' I enquired.

'No, darling, especially for you! You are the ray of sunshine in my life, beautiful inside and out. You really believe in that God of yours, don't you, and that Holy Spirit?'

'I do indeed, Ben, bless you.' I responded.

I never really went to the farm again, nor did I ever telephone an order on Friday, my normal shopping day. When I opened my door to take in the post one day I found a huge box of selected fruit and vegetables on the step. I knew just where it came from. I rang him.

'Ben, that must be you. How much do I owe you, how did you know what I wanted?'

He laughed. 'That Holy Spirit.'

'When did you leave it, Ben?' I asked him.

'Four o'clock, before I drove to Covent Garden market,' he told me.

'Ben, you really must not do that and go out of your way.'

'But you go out of your way for people all the time,'

he replied, 'and don't dare offer to pay for anything I leave.'

I knew he meant it. I knew he was from Jehovah Jireh, so I did not argue. But that was not all.

'Do you eat meat?' he asked me one day.

'Yes, but I rarely buy it.'

'Have you got that old mortgage yet?'

'No, but I shall. My God is faithful,' I told him.

By this time I had taken him to Church and he met my mother, who loved him. His manners were those of a country gentleman. The first time I met him for Church was the first time I saw him in a suit. It was pale blue and he wore a lovely pale blue shirt and tie. His thick silver hair was absolutely shining.

'Why, Ben, you look smart,' I greeted him. I was going to drive him to Hounslow in my car.

'Well, I must be smart with a lovely lady like you,' he said.

He was very puzzled in the Church.

'All that waving and dancing about, darling. We didn't use to do that, and the ladies all wore hats. Do you have a hat?'

'No, Ben, and please don't buy me one,' I implored, for fear that he might!

The boxload of fruit and vegetables was left each week. He always knew what I needed. Then I began to discover steak, yes, real steak under the vegetables, and butter and cheese! Finally I was able to cancel the milkman as milk was left also. This almost became like a Christmas hamper as chocolates and candy were added. Finally I telephoned him.

'Ben, we must talk. Will you please come to the Clinic?' I requested.

We sat down under my front loggia. It was a lovely day. He surveyed the garden. I made him some tea.

34

'Everything is kept so beautiful, just like you. Do you do all the planting yourself?'

'Yes, and I love my garden. The garden is a long story of me replanning it all after my husband left,' I told him.

'Why should a man want to leave anyone like you, Pearl?'

'Well, Ben,' I said, 'there are always two sides to every story, but when I was young and arrogant I thought I could convert an atheist. I married at twenty-three, with stars in my eyes, as a committed Christian but totally ignorant of what the Bible says about marriage. At the time I knew the passage "no two people shall be unequally yoked together" and I discussed it with the vicar of my parish church but he said it would be fine. He told me that "the love of a good woman would save the man" and of course I had no idea that meant when already married.

You see, Ben, I went to Church at the age of three. I was a choir girl, confirmed, a bellringer and a Sunday School teacher, but the most we read the Bible was a few passages on a Sunday. Now I would feel starved if I did not read several chapters every day.'

'Do you understand what it means now?' He asked.

'Not all of it, by any means. I just ask the Holy Spirit to teach me, and the more you read the more you understand. But really, Ben, I have asked you here because I am overwhelmed with your great kindness. I am eating more sumptuously than I have never eaten in my life. I actually cannot consume all that you leave and I have to give some of it away. What is going on? You know there is only one of me to eat all that food.'

'Well, I just want to make sure you have enough. I don't mind if you give it away, for I know you will not waste anything.'

He looked at me very hard.

'Sunshine,' he said, 'has it ever occurred to you that your God might speak to me?'

I felt too moved to speak. I knew I must not say one word more, except to bless him. I cannot imagine what so many others thought as I off-loaded surplus fruit and vegetables on them. They must have thought I was a rotten shopper purchasing above my needs. But truly Ben blessed me, and I was able to bless not a few as a result. For two years my food bill was zero. It was not only that, but I lived off the fat of the land!

I used to say to the Lord, 'Well, Lord, I'm even being fed like the daughter of the King. Thank you, Lord.'

Not only that, but each spring boxes of bedding plants would be left under the porch. Red geraniums – such a price to buy, white alyssum, blue lobelia, multi-coloured pansies and even rose trees. He mended my fences and even painted me a house sign with great skill. He never wanted to come indoors. He was always busy, but that man gave me respect, honour, and treated me like the weaker vessel. I lacked nothing.

'The Lord is my shepherd; I shall not want.'
(Psalm 23:1)

Chapter 6

Ben's Illness

One week there was nothing left under the porch. This did not concern me at all, but I was concerned about Ben. However, I waited another week before I drove to the yard.

I found Ben still piling up neat trays of green grocery, but very ashen. He was wheezing badly.

'Sorry, Sunshine, I couldn't make it.'

'Ben,' I protested, 'you are sick. Have you seen a doctor?'

'Yes, I've got some antibiotics.'

'That's a waste of time, Ben,' I said. 'Now look, you know I'm a clinical practitioner. I want you to come and see me. Let me look after you.'

'No, dear. I thought about that. I would, but my son says you're not a doctor.'

'What on earth has that to do with anything, Ben? Will you come? I'll collect you. It's easier for me to look at you in my consulting room. I believe you have Candidosis. Have you been like this before?'

He told me it happened a lot, those attacks like asthma, and as he was speaking I had a real prompting of the Holy Spirit.

'Ben, I've never seen all of your premises. Could you show me around? What is through that door?'

I indicated a small door at the side of one of the big cowsheds. He told me the place was quite big, that he would show me when he was better. However I insisted it was to be now.

He pushed open the little door and I was led on a tour of a very vast piece of derelict land, pig styes, stables, and sheds housing all manner of rusting agricultural implements. He told me he had raised pigs during the war, and the land was his. He explained it was worth millions and everyone wanted to buy it, but he would not sell because the old farmhouse would have to go with it and he did not want it pulled down. His sons and daughters all wanted him to sell and live with one of them, but he told me they knew he would be unhappy doing so.

We trundled on it seemed, for miles. Often I had to climb over huge piles of crates or lumps of metal. Finally we were making our way back to the main shed when he opened a door in the passage exit to the estate which I had not yet seen, with the words,

'This is where we strip off.'

I stepped inside, grabbing my handkerchief and placing it over my nose and mouth as I stared in disbelief at mounds and mounds of rotting vegetable strippings. It was a paradise for the deadly spores of mycotoxins. Ben must have inhaled them for years. It was a wonder he had survived.

I quickly hustled him out. How was I going to explain to him this dreadful occupational hazard of exposure to moulds? Certainly the time was not now.

I went home, collected all the equipment I could muster and called at the farmhouse. I had never been inside before. Oh, the dust! That poor man, he must have a terrible allergy to house dust mite.

I did the tests as professionally as I could in his sitting room, and left him all manner of vitamins, minerals and instructions. I was crying out to God, 'Please heal him, Lord,' knowing that I couldn't possibly clean the old farm house, or prevent his work stripping off the outsides of vegetables to make them presentable.

As I went backwards and forwards to care for him, I bumped into one of his sons. It was a complete waste of time explaining and I knew it. Here were a family who had sold fruit and vegetables for years, risen at 3.00 am to go to market twice a week, loaded, off-loaded and carted sacks of greengrocery for years.

As he got better and began to smile again he questioned me.

'I think you really care about me, Sunshine.'

'Care, Ben?' I retorted. 'That's an understatement. I love you with the love of Jesus, and I bless you, in His name. I cannot bear the ignorance which has made you so sick. All I can say is that you must be tough to have coped until now. Have you taken your pills today?'

'No, just going to take them.'

'Good, I'll watch you.'

I then suffered a practitioner's nightmare as he washed them all down with whiskey!

'Ben,' I insisted, 'alcohol will stimulate your gut yeasts.'

'Yes, but it makes the vitamins taste good,' he chuckled.

I put my head in my hands in real despair. I knew I had to let it be. Bless him, like me he was a survivor.

Whilst in his sitting room I glanced around at the dusty shelves and furniture. The room was like an antique dealer's dream, housing some incredibly valuable pieces. I couldn't help wondering if he knew what he was sitting on. It was like the den of Midas!

I prayed with Ben, he always liked that, and I departed for the Clinic.

'I'll see myself out, Ben,' I told him.

'No lady sees herself out of my house,' he told me and escorted me to the car.

As I pulled away he asked, 'Sorted out that old mortgage yet, Sunshine?'

'No,' I said, 'but the Lord has it in hand. He's my Jehovah Jireh.'

I drove off into the winter's night, chatting to the Lord as I drove.

'It really is a funny old world, Father. All that land just idling there and enough valuables to raise money for thousands of Jews in destitution.'

Below is reproduced a letter of mine printed in the *Daily Telegraph* 'Letters to the Editor' on 7 January 1985. It explains the problem Ben was facing through dealing with moulds on vegetable humous:

DEAF EARS ON HEALTH WARNINGS

Sir, I refer to Dr Walter Yellowlee's letter on 'the horrific results of pesticides' (Dec. 22); sadly such warnings have fallen on deaf ears over the decades. Thus, the world's immune defence mechanism is undermined by what we are doing to our crops and pastures, and man at the end of the food chain reaps increasing disease from sick soil.

The problem of mycotoxins, fungal poisons in the food chain, is rearing its head in ugly proportions. Mycotoxins are extremely large molecules consisting of oxygen, hydrogen and carbon. They may also contain atoms of nitrogen and chlorine. Once formed they are stable cumulative poisons. These chemicals are difficult to destroy or remove from the food chain.

Modern farming methods based on chemicals and machines have doubled our yield of cereals, but introduced horrifying channels of disease. In wet years it is impossible to dry combine-harvested grain on the farm or at the silo before the fungi have grown, sporulated and produced hosts of mycotoxins. British methods of drying cereals down to a 16 per cent moisture content means that growth of fungi is not inhibited by drying.

The ramifications are endless. It is no wonder that allergy clinics experience vast numbers of patients allergic to cereals. Such patients also invariably have the problem of Candidiasis, now rapidly being called 'the yeast connection', which produces a long list of symptoms with depression, exhaustion and gut disease often uppermost.

Our doctors are often unaware of these problems or how to treat them, and a low mould diet is **vital** to the success of treatment.

At the same time, suggestions are being made for national fluoridation, which means a potent broad spectrum enzyme inhibitor being added to water for the sake of children's teeth when they consume 0.4 per cent of the total public water supply. The 99.96 per cent has to be polluted with an enzymatic poison, in order that children may continue to consume vast amounts of confectionery: again, a devastating, well documented fact which is totally ignored in high places.

The whole environmental picture consitutes one of madness on the part of those who have scientific information under their noses.

Chapter 7

Mortgage or Else!

I received a telephone call from my solicitor asking me if I had found anyone willing to lend me the money with which to buy out my husband. I was to be taken into the high court if I could not buy him out for one third of the market price. The expense of a QC was explained to me and he recommended that we need not incur such an expense.

I had to agree he had done an incredible job for me. The holding operation had allowed the Clinic to be refurnished and, supported by several eminent doctors, it had taken off. I was working full time and economising like crazy to save every penny to reduce the sum I needed to borrow. However I had exhausted all possibilities. Nobody would lend me money because I was not considered a good bet. It seemed very tough.

My solicitor said kindly, 'You had better pray to that God of yours, Mrs Coleman.'

I was praying, and ferreting about for possible sponsors with everything I'd got, believe me. One of my patients started a 'Save the Clinic' fund. I had never begged or tried to raise money with appeals in my life. I hated doing so, but I was eternally grateful for the assistance I did receive. It really blessed me, but was a drop in the ocean.

With three days to go I collected all my books and papers for the umpteenth time and drove to the bank, full of what I was going to say, although I had said it all before.

'Now look here, Mr Bank Manager, I've banked at Barclays since I was fifteen. I have never been in the red, and as you can see from those figures, my income is gradually increasing. Added to this I have invested in equipment worth ... etc., etc., etc.'

Although I had rehearsed these interviews time and again, the end result was always the same. My aged Bank Manager was not at all helpful, although sympathetic.

'So sorry, we cannot help in this instance.'

I was ushered into a side room whilst I awaited the arrival of the Big Chief. He seemed ages coming. I was praying in the Spirit. I needed a lot of money. Suddenly the door opened and a young man popped his head in the door.

'I'm waiting for the Bank Manager,' I explained.

'I am he,' came the response.

'What about Mr Banderlay?' I asked.

'He retired last week. Can I help you?'

Almost breathlessly I poured out my tale of woe. He flicked through my audited accounts as though they were a pack of cards.

'How much do you want?'

I named the sum, my mouth dry with apprehension.

'No problem,' he said. 'When do you want it?'

'Tomorrow.'

'Fine. Pop in and we'll arrange it.'

'Thank you, Father, thank you, Father,' I said aloud as he ushered me out.

As a parting shot he asked, 'What do you actually do?'

I gasped to think he had sanctioned all that money to be loaned without even knowing. I filled him in fast and he was extremely grateful.

Later his very sick wife, a really beautiful lady with severe ulcerative colitis, became my patient and also his mother, who had severe arthritis and was unable to play her cello. Both got quite well, and I thought to myself that the Lord honoured this young bank manager because he blessed the Lord's Clinic. He was their Jehovah Jireh, and they didn't even know it.

So I had this enormous mortgage, and insufficient income to pay it off. But I must not fear or doubt, God was on my side.

When Ben next asked me, 'Got that old mortgage yet, Sunshine?'

I was able to say 'Yes, and my Father owns *the cattle upon a thousand hills'* (Psalm 50:10), and He saw to it.

My former husband paid his last visit to the Clinic to sign the papers we had to exchange. We were civil to each other. When he stepped into the house where he had lived for over twenty years I invited him to sit down and offered him a coffee. He accepted. I sensed him looking round the place with incredulity at what he was seeing. It did look beautiful. I placed the coffee on the little table in front of him.

'What's going on here?' he asked uncomfortably. 'There is something peculiar about this place.'

'It's the Holy Spirit,' I told him.

That dear man, if only he could have shared what I knew, his life would have been so different. But there we are, it is often those closest to us that we fail to help. It's a funny old world, praise the Lord!

So I started these enormous monthly payments and my bank balance dipped dangerously several times. I continued to pray and trust and believe for it being miraculously reduced so I could handle it. To all outward appearances, life for me personally was spartan. But I did not mind. I was so happy in my home and the garden. It was all being made into something beautiful for Him.

I was as busy as a bee in the Clinic and the Ministry. I rarely stopped. Many loving people had gathered around me. My life had real purpose; His purposes for me.

Then in summer, when I was a bit exhausted with my own frugality, something plopped through the letter box one Sunday morning. It was a thick white envelope marked simply 'From Ben'. It was so thick it had been literally stuffed through the letterbox and the envelope was torn.

I gazed in disbelief as a very large wad of notes was revealed. I could not believe it. I rang Ben. He stopped me before I started.

'I don't take orders, only from above.'

I knew absolutely that what he was saying was true. I knew also not to protest. He did, however, tell me that he had wanted to help me so much before I took the mortgage, that he had plenty of money in the bank and building society.

'You see,' he told me, 'I couldn't take it out because they would have wanted to know where it had gone.'

'Who are they, Ben?' I asked.

'My sons. They'll get millions from the land when I die, and the rest, but they would think it odd if I gave you all that money.'

Ben twice repeated his magnificent gesture and the mortgage was dramatically reduced so I could cope with

46

it. I felt so loved and rewarded by my Father. When I would see Ben driving his clapped-out Ford van I used to smile, inside and out. How true that one cannot judge a parcel by the wrapping.

The next time we went to Church together, he insisted that he drove me. I wasn't too happy perched up high with the sliding doors tending to slide open. However I travelled with him to please him. He handed me a bunch of lovely flowers as I climbed in.

'Oh dear,' I thought, 'I must put them in water, but we will be late for Church.'

These thoughts evaporated as he said, 'The flowers are beautiful like you, beautiful inside and out. I suppose if I asked you, you wouldn't marry me, would you, Sunshine? It's just that I'd like to take care of you.'

I forgot the flowers. They dropped on the floor. I put my head down on my lap and I wept. I wept a very great deal. All my life I had longed for someone to appreciate me, to treasure me, to treat me like a lady. Here was this lovely old farmer turned market stallholder, with his noble countenance and hard-worn fingers, gnarled from trimming vegetables in a mouldy spore-infested shed, saying the sweetest things I had ever heard.

'It's just that I'd like to take care of you.'

I thanked him tenderly and blessed him with all my heart. I took his hands.

'Ben, you honour me with your proposal, but you know it is out of the question, but thank you so much anyway.'

He died a few weeks later. I was sure he went to heaven. For sure he was blessed. He was God's provision for me, and actually, though he may not have understood it, he gave me the love of Jesus.

'Blessed is he that blesseth thee.'   (Numbers 24:9b)

'And I will bless them that bless thee and curse them that curse thee.' (Genesis 12:3a)

I did not know then I was of Jewish ancestry.

Chapter 8

Reflections

As I said at the beginning, I'm having a really tough time, and writing these first seven chapters has been extremely beneficial and healing for me.

I've had so much pruning, and I've written three books since the events I have shared with you took place. Judging from the correspondence, thousands have been set free, healed and delivered by reading them. Letters continue to arrive from all over the world. My staff call the books the silent ministry!

The writing of these books caused me to be able to dispense with all advertising. Patients arrive solely as a result of reading them or through recommendation by those who have. Opportunities to minister have come through the same source. I do praise God for all this. Again, it has been His provision.

I truly believe that the Clinic is preparing God's people to cope better in End Times. Much of what we teach here is how people can do without their fixes. I'm not talking about heroin or cocaine, but tea and coffee, sugar and salt, biscuits and cakes, instant junk foods and fizzy drinks, often called 'calorie-controlled' but loaded with poisonous chemicals.

The pressures in today's society causes people to reach out for 'pop in the oven for twenty minutes' meals. Such foods are glued together with additives to increase shelf life and shorten your life. Please be aware of the subliminal manipulation that is going on in the food industry and advertising to persuade us to have a technological feast. Please hear me! These foods artificially raise the blood sugar so that when you are not eating them you feel tired, and the more you consume them the more tired you will become!

A very large proportion of people eat bread (grains) at every meal: Muesli for breakfast with toast, sandwiches or filled rolls for lunch and breaded fish or chicken for supper, etc., etc. Their potassium levels are often virtually non-existent (explanation below) and their sodium levels high. The refined carbohydrate content of their diets makes them sitting ducks for adult-onset diabetes, which is on the increase. All convenience foods are high in both sugars and salt.

Sodium (salt), apart from raising blood pressure, creates unnatural thirst. Realise that all the little dishes of free salted nuts and potato crisps placed at bars in pubs and restaurants are there to make you thirsty. Unfortunately people do not use water to quench their thirst but alcohol, sweetened drinks and tea and coffee.

Tea and coffee are solvents leaching out precious anti-stress factors, like magnesium and calcium, from the body. Alcohol is not only a drying agent, but has a high proportion of sugar and yeast. Water is the only wetting agent. My patients have to drink at least 6–8 glasses a day!

When diabetics come for treatment and I give them a low carbohydrate diet, the first question is,

'What if I have a hypo?'

I tell them they won't, but if they do, two glasses of

water will raise the blood sugar level in seconds. It never fails.

Salt is extremely sinister in its effects on the body. People who consume a high salt diet and do not sweat or weep are in real danger. I want to say something very vital about this, and explain why suppressing grief is really very dangerous, and a luxury no one can afford. It is based on my clinical and ministry experiences over many years and it concerns cancer.

Cancer is often a seed of grief, sown well before the actual visual presentation of the growth. Grief is multifactorial and can be caused by loss, whether of a loved one, a job, a home one loved, money, position or whatever. There are two sorts of people: those who cry and those who do not cry, either because it is physically impossible or (the stoics) because observers are criticising them, telling them to 'snap out of it' before grief has been fully dealt with.

'Don't cry in front of me, I cannot stand it,' can be the accusative cry. Or mourners are made to feel guilty or ashamed in genuine grief because the observer judges them to have wept long enough.

Please beware of judgement upon yourself, if you inflict such vile condemnation upon others. They may not be the 'cissy'. Rather *you* may be the coward unable to take the genuine grief of others. That is *not* like Jesus, who did weep over lost ones.

Hear what I am saying. Our body chemistry when healthy maintains a perfect cellular sodium/potassium balance. The potassium being intra-cellular in the healthy state. The sodium is extra-cellular, in the body fluids, and is released naturally in body secretions, e.g. perspiration, saliva and tears. During stress excess sodium can be produced and needs to be discharged naturally to preserve the healthy internal milieu. Being forced to suppress grief is a major root of cancer in my not inconsiderable experience.

As a child I was a stoic. I was called sunshine or smiler, whatever I was enduring. In my twenties I learned to weep as a safety valve. I am not by nature a weeper but I learned biologically the danger of suppressions. I can weep for others and I often do when ministering. There is no shame in this.

Why then should there be shame in weeping in one's own grief when it is a safety valve? Jesus not only wept, He told those weeping for His sufferings to weep for themselves and their children, for what would come upon them (Luke 23:28). The Amplified version of the well-known Sermon on the Mount renders Luke 6:21:

> *'**Blessed** (happy – with life-joy and satisfaction in God's favour and salvation, apart from your outward condition – and to be envied) are you who **weep and sob now, for you shall laugh!**'*
>
> (emphasis added)

Daniel's mourning for three full weeks not only brought forth one of the greatest revelations in the Bible, but was needed to enable even the mighty angel of God to win through over Satan's opposition to it! (Daniel 10:1–14). Other witnesses of the refreshment, relief and growth that takes place through weeping and mourning are numerous in the Psalms, Job, Lamemtations, and Jeremiah, etc., etc. and include Peter and Paul in the New Testament.

You will hear some ministers tell you that they have ministered to others when they are dying inside themselves. I observe many in ministry carrying on whilst they harboured a spirit of grief and mourning, and it is also known to me that their unshed tears for themselves become a pre-malignancy.

There are some outward signs of the dangers: a misty sodium ring around the iris, a salty taste in the mouth, food can begin to taste salty, blocked sweat ducts, lumps anywhere (especially breast in females), allergy to sodium – which is easily tested, drying up of normally moist membranes, headaches, puffiness of joints, blisters. Remember, the sodium ion has an affinity for the hydrogen ion and excessive saline in tissues can cause water retention

Now please hear what I am saying, not what I am **not** saying. None of these mean you have got cancer, but the warning signs must be dealt with by taking precautions, as you would to avoid any disease.

1. Sodium-free diet (e.g. no added salt).
2. High potassium diet (fresh vegetables and fruit).
3. Take some potassium tablets to help push the salt out.
4. Get deliverance of grief and mourning.
5. Do not suppress tears.
6. Avoid high sodium containing foods, e.g. salted nuts, crisps, kelp, green olives, dill pickles, cheese, some canned fish like tuna and anchovy.

Please do not expect victory by cursing the cancer until the root is dealt with first. People may deny grieving because it is so long ago that someone died or a tragedy occurred. I had quite a nasty experience myself recently.

During recent traumas I developed a dry mouth, dry eye sockets, tremendous allergy to sodium when I have not taken salt for 20 years! I realised that I had been suppressing tears because I thought people were fed up with the traumas in which I was involved. Nasty things began to happen to me, but I felt shame at weeping. That was the Accuser of the Brethren.

Peculiar things happened to my breasts and my uterus. Satan was trying to put cancer on me and I knew it. During a ministry I received from three of the team I spoke of feeling that I had a million unshed tears in my womb. Ladies, the womb can weep, believe me, as you will see from Dulcie's testimony in the next chapter.

I sat in my car one day and became aware of what was happening to me. I used to drive out somewhere to cry. The Lord said to me,

'Weep before me any time, and preferably in your home.'

My father could not cry. He died of cancer, so did his four brothers and sister, a large family of children not allowed to cry! Be warned and informed on this vital issue: do not feel shame in tears, but release! Remember too God's promise,

'Those who sow in tears shall reap in joy.'
(Psalm 126:5)

As a child, did you ever pour salt on a slug or worm and see it dissolve? I am ashamed to say I did. These creatures are pure protein, and sodium destroys them. We too are made of protein. For example our mucous membranes; think about the effect of sodium on them! Do you consider there could possibly be a breaking down of such tissue caused by sodium retention? Well I do, and I've seen patients regenerate from sodium detox-ification alone. Praise the Lord!

Chapter 9

Fibroid Goes in Jesus' Name

Dulcie has been standing with me faithfully for almost a decade. I have seen Jehovah Jireh operating in her life. During her trials of haemorrhage the Lord provided her with two brothers in Christ from the team who had a real burden to stand with her. None of us knew about their faithfulness until it was all over. I will let Dulcie tell you in her own words what happened.

Dulcie's Testimony

'For years I had been weighed down with a heavy menstrual flow each month, which became worse after the birth of our son. I had been told many times by doctors this was normal so I accepted it and carried on as usual. I had few symptoms to complain about, apart from my husband's remarks that I could be quite irritable!

But over the last two or three years I had noticed increasing back pain and tiredness which became almost intolerable. I put this down to the strain of extra work due to house renovations and running Esther House, our Christian guest house in Dover. With threatening despair for our finances due to the Channel Tunnel non-event, things have been extra stressful.

However, it all came to a head in the spring of 1992 when I suffered a haemorrage lasting three weeks. Praise the Lord, He kept me going doing all my work, and I even went on an eight mile prayer walk with friends at the end of the three weeks! But I began to realise the flow was not going to stop of its own accord and I had to see the doctor.

I was crying out to the Lord knowing He could heal me, also knowing that if I went to the doctor he would suggest a hysterectomy which I was totally against. Firstly I did not want to lose any part of my body. Secondly I was fearful, and thirdly I did not want to take several weeks off as this would cause major financial problems at Esther House. The Lord answered my prayers, inasmuch as I was not whisked off to hospital, but treated with drugs and several courses of HRT before finding the type that did not give me excruciating headaches.

During this time the doctor said I ought to have a hysterectomy and get it over with as soon as possible. That which I feared was coming upon me. It was not merely the thought of having to go through it all but many women I knew still experienced problems in spite of the operation. So here I was in the autumn of 1992, after two years in prayer, with the doctor and most of my Christian friends in favour of the operation.

But Pearl and the team were magnificent, and stood on the Word with me, encouraging me to build up my faith. All this conflict was too much for me and I called upon the Lord to heal me. I was so desperate I said it did not matter if I had to go into hospital. "Just heal me any way You like," I cried.

That did it. From that time on when I was able to let

go completely, I experienced a wonderful peace, completely trusting Him to do it His way, rather than my way, whatever the cost. So at last I decided to go through with the tests and subsequent operation if necessary, believing Jesus could and would heal me before the operation, but it would not **really** matter if He did not. I had indeed let go! This was the new foundation on which to build my faith, a new childlike trust as He took my hand and led me through.

It was a few days before Christmas 1992 that I went to the doctor to arrange the appointment with the hospital for tests. These were carried out in early January 1993. I had never believed it was cancer so when the scan revealed fibroids it was no surprise. But I praise God that's all it turned out to be.

The spiritual battle was on as never before. Two brothers in the team fed me with many Scriptures, much encouragement and prayers as a special burden for me was laid upon them and, praise the Lord, I could feel the support of them all. I was continually fighting the negative talk still surrounding me, like one person who said they never really believed I'd get well until I had a hysterectomy.

When the appointment was made for me in mid-January I knew that I was not ready to confront the consultant. It was changed to February and although the prayer warfare was still raging I knew I needed more time. I changed the appointment yet again to March and the receptionist remarked, "Are you sure you want this appointment?" I cried out that I did. I knew the Lord could and would heal me before they were able to operate. Even as I believed, so it was.

A few days before I was due to visit the consultant I was talking to a lovely Christian lady who said to me "I thought I was healed too but still had to have the operation." The words swirled around my head and I felt as if a knife had been thrust into my gut. I could not believe that all those weeks of prayer and building up could be dashed down by those few words. Pray as I might, I could not rid myself of this horrific wound.

I knew I needed to speak to Pearl. I also knew she had been involved in heavy warfare against Hinduism in Malaysia, and was loathe to worry her on her arrival home. However, I decided to send her a note informing her of the hysterectomy with which I was threatened, and of course to welcome her home after the battle.

She rang me upon receipt of my letter and there was such an anointing over the telephone! There had been many words of knowledge before, and although I cannot remember the content of these prayers they were as a two-edged sword, wonderfully freeing.

The power of the anointing came down the phone line and I drank it all in, that by His stripes I **was** healed. I was given some Scriptures to read as I went to bed, and was at peace. Hallelujah!

Later that night I awoke. This was most unusual as I always sleep very well. I felt most uncomfortable. It was so cosy and warm in bed and I did not relish the thought of getting out. However, I could not understand the nature of feeling so uncomfortable. It felt as though I had had an accident in bed! I reluctantly got out.

To my surprise and delight, I knew the healing had taken place and the intruding fibroids had been expelled and ejected! It was all so neat. I praised the Lord as I cleaned up. I felt so wonderful and was soon asleep again. He gives His Beloved rest!

In the morning I could not wait to tell everyone the great miracle that had taken place. The next two days I rested as much as possible, feeling distinctly postoperative. The next morning, the third day, was the date set to see the consultant.

I was the first patient and was really excited. We were all praying that he would accept what I was to tell him. The Lord does not do anything by halves. A lovely Christian prophetess stayed overnight, en route from the Clinic at Woking, and was able to pray for me as I set out for the hospital in the morning and she returned to Switzerland.

I read my Bible while I waited to be called. I did not want to be talked into having the operation. I need not have worried. The Lord prepared the path. A few questions and answers and his "That's fine" attitude made me feel I should pile on the symptoms. He then amazed me by saying, "No problems, they will all melt away."

I burst out laughing and said they already had by the power of prayer in Jesus' name. He looked at me and replied "Well, that is wonderful. We will see you in six months' time to check all is well." I duly went back and was signed off.

Before I left I explained how the Lord had healed me, in front of four nurses who were in the consulting room and they all listened intently. On both occasions as I left the consulting room I floated out with such joy that my Saviour was also my Healer and Deliverer. And on each occasion my joy turned to compassion as I saw a sea of depressed and sickly looking patients waiting for their turn. I thought if only they knew Jesus, if only they would stop rejecting Him.

Thank you, Jesus, for those faithful intercessors who did not give in after months of prayer, but stayed the course without ceasing. There is no doubt in my mind that without that continual love and support I would not have received the miracle, but would have ended up on the operating table! May we all learn to lay down our lives for each other in the spiritual battle.

What a lesson those past months had been. Letting go, having faith as in Hebrews 11:1, trusting the promises for healing for the here and now for **me**, getting into the right place with God and meeting the conditions of the promise. In the end we have to take responsibility for ourselves, no one can do it for us. Keep on praising, whatever the circumstances. As I travelled home I was so grateful, so full of joy with thankfulness. How our heavenly Father looks after us in every situation.'

Dulcie is a very special sister in Christ, who has shown me a love and faithfulness which has been nothing short of steadfast. She is one of the people I would be very happy to have around in the End Times. Full of laughter, joy of the Lord, and a very special discernment and wisdom.

Like most of us she came out of the pit of hell, despair, and all manner of agony, and truly she had emerged as a butterfly out of a chrysalis into somebody very different from the scriptural 'old man' she has put off! When I received her letter upon my arrival home, and a subsequent apologetic cry for help because she knew how things had been for me, I felt it urgent to contact her on the telephone.

'Now look here, Dulcie,' I told her, 'I'm fed up with this attack on your body! We've all been praying and standing with you, and Satan is not going to get away with this. Hysterectomy, my foot!' Together we prayed in agreement, and indeed the anointing was strong. I suddenly found myself coming against a 'weeping womb' and 'the tears of Rachel who wept for her children and refused to be comforted.' I commanded the fibroid to be dispersed in Jesus' name.

Dulcie felt very tired after the ministry and I told her to lie down and sleep. Her husband, dear Ron, had been standing with her and agreed with me. Well, you have read Dulcie's testimony and that fibroid was expelled in the name of Jesus Christ, literally cut out with the sword of the Spirit. In the name of Jesus it had to go. I believe this testimony will encourage other women with similar problems.

All glory goes to the Lord Jesus Christ.

Chapter 10

Ministry to Asians

Earlier readers will know that I have been very involved, one way or another, in ministry to Asians, both here and abroad. I have a very genuine love for Chinese, Malays and Indians (possibly because of ancestral associations with India), and I have also ministered to countless Africans.

Apart from the deep love I bear these brothers and sisters in Christ, I find they are extremely receptive to the ministry of deliverance. They understand evil spirits because their ancestors have usually been involved in witchcraft. I am very, very happy ministering in these groups.

My spirit sometimes really empathises with them. It's difficult to describe, but it's definitely there. Particularly in Malaysia, observing the radiance of these people in worship, their spontaneity and response to the Holy Spirit, I have been aware that underneath all their joy is a deep, deep sadness and sense of loss.

Since I started to minister to those nationalities some ten years ago, I have been more and more convinced and led by the Holy Spirit to believe an ancestral devourer in their lives robs them of the complete victory. Many,

many times I see them join prayer lines, respond to altar calls for they don't know what.

When I am a member of a conregation where this happens, at home or abroad, I can hardly contain myself from rushing up front and saying,

'Let me lead you in this prayer for freedom of ancestral curse, and let's put an end to all this deception and cover-up.'

I am so aware too of the link between the New Age Movement and these religions and cults. The multi-faith horror we are seeing birthed everywhere is strongly dominated by Hinduism and the New Age. Don't let anyone persuade you otherwise.

Of course, multi-faith is just one aspect of the perilous times in which we are living right now, just as one-world government, one-world currency and the one-world bible are. That bible, please note is not the Holy Bible in which you will read the whole Word of God, as many of the most important bits are left out.

During the warfare in which I have been engaged of late two passages of the Scripture have weighed so heavily upon me.

> *'This know also, that in the last days perilous times shall come. For men shall be lovers of their own selves, covetous, boasters, proud, blasphemers, disobedient to parents, unthankful, unholy. Without natural affection, trucebreakers, false accusers, incontinent, fierce, despisers of those that are good. Traitors, heady, highminded, lovers of pleasures more than lovers of God; Having a form of godliness, but denying the power thereof: from such turn away.'* (2 Timothy 3:1–5)

Also Matthew 10:34–39:

'Think not that I am come to send peace on earth: I came not to send peace, but a sword. For I am come to set a man at variance against his father, and the daughter against her mother, and the daughter in law against her mother in law. And a man's foes shall be they of his own household. He that loveth father or mother more than me is not worthy of me: and he that loveth son or daughter more than me is not worthy of me. And he that taketh not his cross, and followeth after me, is not worthy of me. He that findeth his life shall lose it, and he that loseth his life for my sake shall find it.'

These words have been bitter in my belly, and if you cannot understand the difference between honey in the mouth and bitter in the belly, Ezekiel 3, please make it your business to listen to the exposition of that chapter by Yacov Prasch (available through Moriel Ministries, 95 High Street, Yeadon, Leeds LS19 7NP). If you listen to this powerful revelation and do not fall on your face groaning in your spirit, you are lukewarm (Revelation 3:15–16)!

The words in verse 34 of Matthew 10 made me aware of what I am involved in, having received so many revelations for Asians during the last four years. My spirit was stirred about such things when I had someone staying at the Clinic with me for about eighteen months, whose ancestors were Hindu Tamils.

The Lord had laid a strong commitment to this gentleman, whom I will call Joshua, on my heart way back in 1989. It was a commitment through which I learned so much, that I could not envisage any other way in which I could have gained such knowledge and understanding of what people with such ancestry are up against.

For example, I was not aware at the time that the swastika was a Hindu symbol or sign. I had noticed, however, that this very dear man extolled everything made in Germany, whether it was cars, washing machines or refrigerators. We discovered the spirit behind German pride and idolatry, and specifically the Aryan origins claimed by Hitler and Nazism, is also a spirit of India, and that they both go back to Babylon! So this interest was not as strange as it might seem.

As a television addict, his passion for war films in which German soldiers were portrayed was very marked. He would eulogise over every detail of their military uniforms, even to the stitching of the leather pouches for their Luger pistols, and gaze at them as a person totally mesmerised.

I was often disquieted by what he was watching and would ask him to switch it off. He always did this, but accompanied by sighs of protest or even rude remarks. Upon many occasions this created an atmosphere of hostility. It was part of a greater spiritual warfare that was raging below the surface.

Yet I always felt that here was a man God wanted to use and that deep inside him was the capability of strong and faithful love and loyalty, plus a desire to serve the Lord, which was being frustrated by demonic activity of every kind. I had no doubt that Satan had used this man mightily in the past and was reluctant to let him go.

I was always convinced he was a man of God, chosen to be a warrior for Christ, a man of intense strength and potential to bring the unsaved to the Lord. I never lost sight of the vision the Lord had given me through His spirit for a special task He had for this man, even before he was in his mother's womb.

Precious friends around me, including my 'family', the team, grew weary sometimes of the wranglings that went on, and his seeming inability to grasp God's almighty hand to freedom. There was no doubt that what was in him hated me, and was doubly restless in the sanctuary of the Clinic where it was challenged daily by the anointing of the Holy Spirit.

As a young man he had been robbed of twelve precious years of his life by heroin addiction and involvement in martial arts in Pakistan, and had come to the Clinic for detoxification and healing. He grew extremely fit and started to attend a local gymnasium to do some exercise to strengthen his muscles. One morning when he was going to the gym I took the bull by the horns, challenging him that he idolised the Germans.

To my astonishment he replied,

'You could have a point, Pearl. I think everything German is excellent and superior, that they have the smartest uniforms, and did you see in Penang how I greet my friends?'

'No,' I said.

He raised his right arm in a Nazi salute and said,

'Seig heil,' then laughed and continued, 'Didn't you ever see me do that? I always greet my friends that way.'

'No, I certainly did not, because had I done so I would have jumped on you. Never let me hear you say that again.'

'I'll pray about what you have said' he told me, and left for the gym with a happy wave and smile.

'The curse of the swastika,' I said to myself, as he turned off up the lane.

A few weeks later, during another time of black moods, I offered to buy him some strong, real leather boots like mine. I liked to walk long and hard, and his boots from Malaysia were too light for this, as they were not really walking boots at all.

Frankly, he didn't want to walk. He could not share

my passion for trees and hedgerows, skipping lambs or rippling brooks and orange sunsets over meadows. As we walked I would praise God for every beautiful scene, and point out foliage and berries, extolling their colour and marvelling at the preciseness of God's handiwork. The greatest response I ever drew to what I pointed out with such joy was 'Yes.' I got so bored with his non-reactions to what for me was a beautiful view or land-scape, or the delight of a blackbird in a bush against a pale sky.

Yet in spite of this hardness for creation he once collared my anthology of poems and took it to his room to read, only to emerge weeping because he was so touched by what he read. Also, sometimes when he was angry I would read the Psalms over him and he would weep. This happened on more than one occasion. It was a genuine response.

I also saw his spirit touched by certain desperately ill or possessed patients who came to the Clinic, and he brought not a few people to the Lord both in the Clinic and outside in the street. He had the makings of an evangelist, of that I had no doubt. He also had a compassion for the ugly and unloved.

Anyway, he was reluctant to have decent boots bought for him, as much as I was determined that he would not sit in leisure time watching the TV, but get out and walk with me! If I went out and walked alone, I could be sure to return and find him glued to the set.

Chapter 11

The Boots

One bright and crispy morning we were finally off to Guildford in search of real boots. I didn't care what they cost, real walking boots were a ten-year investment, at least. We should only want one pair, as the Lord would surely be here before they wore out! I had paid £100 for mine, and that was five years previously. My former pair at twelve years of age are now supporting someone else's feet in Israel, praise the Lord!

Well, you would have thought that my friend had asked me for bread and I was giving him a stone. He shambled in and out of shops, looking down his nose at everything he tried on, being totally disenchanted with whatever weary shop assistants brought him.

He was also more than reluctant to put on the thick walking socks needed to test such boots out. He was about as co-operative as a mule and his black eyes looked really hard and evil. There were days when I felt I quite disliked him. He was moody, sullen and totally unpleasant.

'What on earth am I doing wasting my time on this one for?' I asked myself, as he reluctantly laced up another pair of very expensive walking boots.

He was also sensing my exasperation as I said 'Well?'

He shuffled uncomfortably around the shop, determined not to like the boots. I could have kicked him up the pants!

'You ungrateful oaf,' I thought. 'Well?' I asked again.

'Alright' he answered.

'Alright, what?' I questioned.

I felt sorry for the assistant who had been backwards and forwards to produce something he approved of. Now I was cross.

'You do not like them, do you? Come on then, get them off and we'll go.'

I apologised to the assistant, rather pathetically, that it was a bad day and we went downstairs to the lower shop. It was a sports shop with shoes upstairs. As we commenced to leave the premises I paused to look at some shirts hanging near the exit when I noticed he was glued to the side window by the door, just inside the entrance. His face was lit up.

'Well?' I enquired crossly.

He was gazing at some very high black leather boots which fastened well above the ankle.

'Oh,' he said, 'Look, Pearl, at the soft leather and all those lovely studs to take the laces. They are beautifully made.'

I looked at them and told him they would take ages to lace up, but it was clear that he really was taken by them.

'They are only £25,' he said.

I screwed up my face in disbelief and pushed my nose against the window. I thought they looked a bit old fashioned but they were certainly leather with good strong soles, and if this bad-tempered, unappreciative oaf desired boots for £25, instead of around £100, well then that suited me fine!

Up the stairs we trekked again. The dismayed lady shop assistant avoided us like the plague and a man came to serve us. I was apologetic, explaining that my friend had seen his heart's desire in the window. Did they have size $8\frac{1}{2}$? The man said yes and went behind the scenes to produce the boots. His other shoes were already off, the walking socks on and his feet waiting!

He almost purred as he put the boots on, commenting on how beautifully made they were, stroking the leather. Dear me, it seemed to take an eternity to lace them up, but he was quite happy to painstakingly crisscross and tighten the laces well over the ankles. Next to my chunky walking boots they looked like boots for a ballerina! He trod around the shop in undisguised glee, approving of every step he took.

'Why are they only £25?' I asked the man, who clearly believed they were sold to the Malaysian prancing round the shop. I froze where I sat as the reply came straight and clear.

'They are recycled German paratroopers boots, Madam.'

'Holy Spirit!' I entreated.

I looked at my pal; what was in him looked back at me. It was confrontation time!

'Wisdom, Lord,' I entreated.

We left the shop with his prized boots. He was not interested in further shopping – just to get home and polish the boots until they shone like glass. This from the most reluctant shoe-cleaner I knew!

Then Ernest brought round a coat he thought would be suitable for our friend in wet weather. We hadn't yet kitted him out with a weatherproof jacket, although frankly there was little he hadn't been bought to provide a wardrobe par excellence, including a beautiful plain

71

burgundy blazer and a dark navy, reefer-type winter coat.

The jacket Ernest handed over was dark olive green military style with a black fur collar. He was out on the courtyard with Ernest when he slipped it on. His eyes were like saucers. We both knew it was like a German officers' military overcoat. He spoke this fact out and, as he said it, mimicked a Nazi officer. He was striding up and down and was just going to raise his hand and salute when he caught my eyes.

'Be bound,' I was saying under my breath as he spoke out.

'Oh, I hadn't better do that.'

'No, you hadn't.' I said.

At this stage Ernest knew nothing about the boots. Later I shared with him and the team. We all could see the funny side of it, especially Dulcie who is such a happy breath of fresh air. She couldn't stop laughing.

'We'll have to curse them, or what's been in them, when he's out,' she said.

That's exactly what we did, except about six of us were cursing not only the spirit in the boots but in all his clothes when he appeared, out of the blue, back at the Clinic! At the next team meeting, when we were in full strength to minister to a couple involved in a cult, I challenged him.

'How about my breaking this curse of the swastika over you, and you repenting of the idolatry?' I asked.

He agreed and this was done, following which, without any pressure, he asked me to get rid of the boots. The coat went out to the garage and I would loan it to dripping wet workmen on very wet days. I saw him walk in complete freedom from that curse.

My secretary Ruth, read Philosophy, Politics and Economics at Oxford and is an informal Bible student, for which she has also done a night class in Hebrew over the last 10 years. She was given the name Ruth by the Lord, and its meanings include (associate with another as) friend, or companion, and is from the root 'to tend or pasture a flock', i.e. feed, herd, shear, pastor, shepherd, and that is exactly what she has been to me.

She found that Nazi Aryanism goes back to Babylon, which relates to End Time prophecies as well, so I asked her to do some notes on it for me and they are below. I see constantly the combination of martial arts, drug addiction and astrological prognostication, but I'll come to that later.

Babylon, Origin of Nazi Aryanism

'*Aryan*' is a Sanskrit (old Hindu scripture) word meaning 'nobles'. The first nobles were Cush and Nimrod, son and grandson of Noah's unrighteous son Ham,

> '*And Cush begat Nimrod; he began to be a mighty one in the earth. He was a mighty hunter before the Lord; wherefore it is said, Even as Nimrod the mighty hunter before the Lord. And the beginning of his kingdom was Babel, and* ... (3 other cities).'
> (Genesis 10:8–10a)

'Before the Lord' also means 'against the Lord'. Cush, followed by his wife Semiramis and son Nimrod, started rebelling against God after the flood. They 'ennobled' themselves, becoming great hunters, warriors, builders, rulers, eventually idols, worshipped and obeyed as gods.

Genesis 11:3-9 tells us they built a city and tower 'to reach heaven, to make a name for themselves, and preserve their unity lest they be scattered'. But God did not wish them to achieve 'all they imagined to do' (including tryanny and abominations) and so scattered them, each with a different language, 'abroad upon the face of the whole earth'.

They of course took their culture with them, which is how Babylonian religion and practices became the basis of others throughout the world, even to the present. The only exception to this is scriptural Judeo-Christianity, which God gave to the Jews to preserve His truth in the earth, and it alone has always **proven** itself true through the accurate fulfilment of hundreds of its own prophecies.

The Aryans geographically are the peoples of North India. Their religion and culture, including Hinduism and Buddhism, originated in Babylon, as did those of the Nazis! When Hitler talked about re-establishing the Aryan super-race in Germany, he was referring ultimately to the Babylonian leaders or 'gods'. But if Babylon was in ancient Persia, how could the idolised Nazi super-race have blond hair and blue eyes, etc., rather than darker features of the Middle East?

Cush and his son Nimrod were negroid in feature (as portrayed in Buddha statues even today). Although worshipped for their great might and abilities, they were evidently personally unattractive, cruel, tryannical and greatly feared. On the other hand, Cush's wife Semiramis had blue eyes, blonde hair, awesome beauty and perhaps even more to the point, she outlasted and replaced them both.

After Cush died, Semiramis married her son Nimrod! He was eventually judicially executed by Shem (Noah's righteous son) for his abominations, including human, even child, sacrifice. However, Semiramis maintained and strengthened her rule by claiming that one of her similarly-featured offspring, from her literally innumerable 'whoredoms', was Nimrod reborn or reincarnated as 'the sun god Baal'.

The child's name was Tammuz and the 'T', at that time written as a cross (crucifix), became a symbol used in his worship and as a good luck charm on buildings, clothing and jewelry etc. It was not originally a Christian symbol at all, but common in heathen religions, and only in the third century AD came into Europe from Egypt, where Christianity was often mixed with Egyptian worship!

So Semiramis became the central image of Babylonian worship, 'Queen of Heaven', 'Virgin Mother of the Child', Madonna, etc., with a list of names and titles running into thousands (the origin of religious litanies), even though it was nominally of Baal (also worshipped under endless different names)! Babylon is in fact portrayed as a woman in Revelation (Chapters 17 and 18).

Another question: if the man/god allegedly being worshipped never existed, Tammuz not being Nimrod, and not worshipped as himself at all, who **was** in fact being worshipped, giving inspiration and power to the system? Revelation 17:5 says:

> 'I will tell thee the mystery of the woman and of the beast that carrieth her, which hath the seven heads and the ten horns. The beast that thou sawest was, and is not and shall ascend out of the bottomless pit, and go into perdition . . . '

The beast that carried the woman of Babylon which ascends out of the bottomless pit is Satan. This is stated clearly in Revelation 2:12–13 which describes the spirit of Pergamos, to which the priesthood and religion moved after Babylon's decline:

> *'And to the angel of the church in Pergamos write:*
> *". . . I know thy works and where thou dwellest, even*
> *where Satan's seat is . . . where Satan dwelleth."'*

So according to Scripture, Babylonianism is Satan worship and he has a seat and dwelling place wherever his worship is established. Interestingly, there was also a particular big black stone brought from Babylon to Pergamos still regarded by some satanists as his visible seat or dwelling place on earth, which Hitler transported to Germany, and Stalin took to Russia at the end of the second World War!

In Babylon, Satan first received worship in the form of Nimrod/Tammuz, as Lucifer, *'the light-bringer'* (Isaiah 14:12). Semiramis had claimed she was Aurora ('the morning') mystically and virginally 'pregnant with light' when she gave birth to Tammuz, supposedly Nimrod reincarnated and thus the 'enlightener' of the souls (minds) of men.

God had promised mankind a deliverer (Genesis 3:15). Nimrod/Tammuz was allegedly this deliverer, bringing the 'enlightenment' or knowledge (actually of sin, rebellion against God, exaltation of human abilities, all forms of evil, the occult, etc.) that Satan told Eve would make men 'as gods' (Genesis 3:5)! He was only the first after the great flood of many anti(e)-Christs (meaning before, in place of, or against Christ), the counterfeit saviours of mankind whose final form is so horrifically described in Revelation. Yacov Prasch points out that prophecy is **primarily pattern, not prediction** and that it occurs repeatedly in many forms, times and places throughout history, although it may indeed have a single final and complete fulfilment.

After Semiramis and Tammuz, the kings of Babylon continued receiving this personal worship as Lucifer

(Isaiah 14:12) and religious leadership under the specific title of 'Supreme Pontiff'. This is **historically** the same title and role claimed by the Supreme Pontiff or Pope in Rome today! After the Babylonian dynasty ended, the priesthood, with its training centre, moved to Greece and conferred the title on the king of Pergamos. After he died it was given to Julius Caesar, and successive Roman Emperors claimed the same worship as gods (Lucifer, but now referred to as Zeus, Jupiter, etc.), persecuting scriptural believers and all who refuse to bow the knee, a common re-occurrence till the end of the age.

Constantine's 'Christianisation' brought little more than Christian names to the pagan gods of the Roman empire. For example, worship of Semiramis under her titles of 'Queen of Heaven', 'Holy Virgin', 'Madonna', 'Mother of the Child' etc., continued under the name of Mary but had little to do with the biblical mother of Jesus. In the Gospels Jesus Himself always refuses (at least publicly) to use the word 'mother' when referring to His human mother Mary, even when others used it directly to Him (Matthew 12:48–50 and 19:29, Mark 3:33–5 and 10:29, Luke 8:21).

Most pointedly of all, when giving Mary into John's care on the cross Jesus called her only *'Woman'* and *thy* (John's) *mother'* (John 19:27). His teaching emphasized that, firstly, His Father in heaven and, secondly, His disciples on earth were the focus of His attention and devotion. Our earthly parents and family we must honour but love less than the Him or the Father (Luke 14:26 and John 14:9), and they would even become our enemies for His sake (Matthew 10:35–7).

In the Babylonian system (as in Nazism and all false religion, secular or spiritual) there was a great deal of deception, destruction and death behind the worship of all things supposedly good and beautiful, such as life, riches, enlightenment, human abilities and strength (physical and mental), nature (sun, animals, trees, rocks, fire, etc.), in fact practically everything but the one true God:

> *'Babylon the great is fallen ... all nations have drunk of the wrath of her fornication, and the kings of the earth have committed fornication with her, and the merchants of the earth have waxed rich through the abundance of her delicacies ... Come out of her my people, that ye be not partakers of her sins, and that ye receive not of her plagues ... How much she hath glorified herself and lived deliciously, so much torment and sorrow give her.'*
>
> (Revelation 18:2–7)

Nimrod was the first king, conqueror and totalitarian ruler after the flood, extending his rule as far as Libya in North Africa. He developed methods for training animals and then men, in skills of hunting and warfare – the first military or martial arts – becoming so seemingly almighty and fearsome it was a great shock to all when he came to a violent but just end himself.

To cover over that fact, Semiramis organised great annual lamentations for his death and celebrations of his alleged rebirth, thereby originating traditions and practices such as Lent, Passion week (including the self/ flagellation), Good Friday, Easter, not to mention the soprano voice, choral and chant singing for religious music!

To avoid any similar end herself, Semiramis also developed the first methods of systematic (political) control through religion, using secrecy, deception, sorcery, group power and force. She formed the first 'priesthood' of 'illumined ones' who alone should understand the higher forms of knowledge, both natural sciences and supernatural 'Mysteries' or mysticism, (occult divination, astrology, spiritualism, etc.) and hence control information and resources to (and from) the people.

As well as idolatry, élitism, religious-political ceremonies, pageantry and festivals (which included orgies, alcohol and drug abuse) to rally and maintain popular support, there were required rituals (public and secret), initiations and 'sacraments', e.g. infant baptism, ordination of priests, sacrifices, confession: willing (auricular) or unwilling (torture), and enforced conformity through persecution. Fertility rites required celibacy for the priest/esses but allowed, even encouraged, homosexuality and promiscuity, such as temple prostitution and 'free love', for the masses. This directly undermined God's system of true independence, stability, order, authority and (generally) fulfilment in family and marriage.

The origin of 'Christmas' was the orgiastic celebration of the 'rebirth' of Molech (meaning 'king') at the winter solstice or 'rebirth of the sun'. As sun god he was worshipped with fire, e.g. bonfires, burning crosses (sometimes with human sacrifices), walking on fire, candles – in temples and on trees, etc. In its worst form, which unhappily was the origin of 'Father Christmas', Molech was not the giver but the receiver of gifts. These were not made to children, but of children, given by their parents as sacrifices to be burnt on the huge stomach of his idols!

However, Yacov Prasch points out that even those abominations never approximated the scale of child sacrifice today, in the form of non-medically essential abortions. These occur not only in the fires of our hospital incinerators but also continually within the uterus of hundreds of millions of women using what is in fact post-conception, aborting forms of so-called 'contraception', such as the coil. Modern sacrifices are made to idols of *'our own ways'* (Isaiah 53:9) such as economic convenience, even in relatively well-off and 'Christian' countries.

Do we need to confess, repent and plead for mercy and conversion on behalf of our authorities and fellow-citizens, as well as ourselves when we do not bear witness to God's strong Words against murder and mistreatment of the poor and innocent? At least we should not wonder or complain when we receive the consequences, for, as Prasch says, if God does not avenge this ever-increasing 'bloodbath' He becomes increasingly unjust to the defenceless and innocent in favour of the able and guilty.

Cahna-Bal, the ancient Celtic Druid Priest of Baal, gives us the word 'cannibal'. Biblical Mosaic law, in which animal sin-offerings to God were afterwards given as food to the priests, was perverted in Babylon into the priest/ess eating human sacrifices to their gods. This is the historical origin and basis of the theory of 'transubstantiation': eating human flesh or a bread substitute sacrificed to a god, allegedly to acquire some of that god's divinity.

This Babylonian system spread from Greece to Rome, and from there to Germany and the rest of Europe. It formed the basis of unbiblical beliefs and practices throughout history, including all Catholic and Christian ones based on the teachings-become-traditions of men rather than Scripture alone. It is flooding back today even into former scriptural strongholds, and the basis of the final one-world religion and government.

Humanism, new age 'alternative' practices, transcendental meditation, martial arts, yoga, etc. coming into education, 'fitness' and management training are all a part of this. So is 'emphasising the common factors between all religions', gradually getting rid of anything on which people disagree, most especially the scriptural Jesus, for the sake of unity.

A main aim of Babylon was unity (Genesis 11:4), under its leadership, of course. Interestingly, 'Catholic' actually means 'universal', so Roman Catholic means Roman Universal. There are estimates of 68 million victims of the Inquisition enforcing Catholicism universally in Europe in the Middle Ages. All who will not comply with the one-world religion worshipping the final Anti-Christ are again eliminated, and as Revelation 18:24 says of Babylon:

> 'In her was found the blood of prophets, and of saints, and of all that were slain upon the earth.'

One Bible scholar says Babylon stands for any form of religion, for all are false, and that means every murder ever committed is due to religion, from Cain downwards! True belief in Jesus is not a religion at all but a personal relationship.

The good news for faithful believers (in the Jesus of the King James Bible) is that persecution will be a major route to heaven before God's judgement and wrath is out-poured on those remaining on earth, who will be made to worship the final anti-Christ. These will condone and cooperate in the persecution of believers to escape from persecution themselves, but instead face what the Bible describes as a time worse than anything known before, even such that

> 'In those days shall men seek death, and shall not find it; and shall desire to die, and death shall flee from them.'   (Revelation 9:6)

81

This is a grim but ultimate reminder and encouragement to believers, that there is no profit or salvation through man or Satan, only in faithfulness to the scriptural Jesus alone.

* * *

Background information is from the well-recommemded classic *The Two Babylons* by Rev. Alexander Hislop (published by S.W. Partridge & Co.); Yacov Prasch's tape series *The 7 Churches of Revelation* (available from Moriel Ministries, 95 High Street, Yeadon, Leeds LS19 7NP), and library encyclopedias. Barry Smith's books give updated information re: Revelation (distributed by Alpha Omega Ministries UK, Suite 1, 1st Floor, Mill Court, Newport, Isle of Wight PO30 2AA. Tel: (0983) 525503).

Chapter 12

Astrological Prognostications

Both Hindus and Chinese have astrological prognostications made over them at birth, and invariably a birth chart of their zodiac sign will be made and even updated annually. The repercussions for Europeans 'following the stars' are bad enough, as I know well, but I feel that for the Indian and Chinese they are even more grave, if that were possible. The real horror of all this first dawned on me spiritually during a very unexpected ministry at Joshua's sister's house, where I stayed for a few days during a visit to Malaysia.

That particular day dawned with the morning stillness disturbed only by the chirping of birds that one experiences in Malaysia. I always feel that later in the day the birds are too hot to chirp at all!

I popped downstairs to make a coffee and grab some papaya. One day I'll write a poem in praise of papaya! Joshua said his mother virtually lived on it and I was happy to do the same. The enzymes in that luscious fruit have a miraculuous quality for the digestive system.

Outside my room was a large square landing, which housed a second TV for the children and cushions for them to sit on. You can imagine how much I disapproved of that! There was also an ironing board, iron and an overspilling laundry box in the other corner.

I paused on the landing to greet Joshua's very beautiful sister who was ironing. I never saw a woman work so hard looking after three children, working full time and being busy for her Church. She was a very special sister in Christ to me already. She always looked so fresh and exquisitely feminine, yet she had no maid and when at home, seemed always to be catching up on household chores.

I bade her good morning and was about to descend the stairs when the Lord said to me,

'Tell her I love her.'

I turned in my tracks and approached her. She paused from her ironing. I placed my hand on her shoulder and gave her the Father's simple message.

To my absolute amazement she collapsed in my arms weeping copiously. Or was I amazed? No, in truth I could not say that was the case, but I suppose it was the unexpected timing of what happened. As always in ministry, it was God's timing, but I had sensed an agony in her before. I took her into my bedroom. She was weeping profusely, deeply and bitterly.

'Darling,' I said, 'wait, I must minister to you.'

I left the room, hung over the banister and shouted, 'Joshua, come quickly.'

In a few moments a somewhat dishevelled and astonished Joshua was at my side, asking what on earth was the matter.

'Your dear sister has a terrible spirit of grief and mourning,' I told him. 'Stand with me.'

I didn't even know if he really understood what was happening, he was so dazed and shocked at this well-controlled sister's complete breakdown.

I opened the Bible, grabbed my olive oil and got

84

cracking. There was not a great deal of space in the room so I stood her facing the window, her back to the side of the bed.

I came against the spirit of grief and mourning and an unbelievable scream rent the air as she slumped forwards and sat down on the edge of the bed, with Joshua and I steadying her. As she screamed, I was staggered to receive the words 'astrological prognostication'.

At the same time I saw that the Kundalini was curled at the base of her spine. This is the Hindu serpent to which is attributed power and life-force strength. It can be as it were dormant, and when angered or roused into its most powerful form, can be spiritually discerned coming out of the top of the back of the head. One sees many Hindu portraits and paintings depicting this effect. The serpent appears always to be a cobra, which is worshipped by Hindus of course.

I was astonished to see this serpent, although it was not a large one, coiled at the base of the spine of a Born Again, Spirit-filled, holy handmaiden of the Lord, for that indeed is what this precious sister was.

Between sobs she was explaining to me that her father, a non-practising Hindu, had birth charts made for all his children at birth. She had only found them recently when clearing out the family home prior to its sale, and had insisted to her mother, also Joshua's mother of course, that they must be destroyed. Joshua's mother was a sweet, devout Christian lady, with a simple and deep faith.

I realised then all this had to be dealt with in Joshua! I asked if he had been into the signs of the zodiac. He informed me that he had, and also that he was greatly influenced by them. He told me he was Pisces, the fish that swims in two directions.

As the Holy Spirit was rapidly processing information

into my spirit, I was realising what a hornets' nest was to be uncovered. I was under the anointing, it was a powerful one, and I moved rapidly to take the land. Before I did this I discerned that the idolatry of Hinduism had never been confessed and repented, not only in this sister but in the whole family! Hosea 4:6 certainly applied!

This being done, I cut the Kundalini in the name of Jesus Christ and came against every astrological prognostication made over her life, cutting her off from every god of air, fire and water, and decommissioning the activity of every curse and every spirit of curse in her life.

She smashed backwards on the bed. I grabbed the oil and anointed her head, declaring

'It's the anointing that breaks the yoke.'

She suddenly lunged forward. The screams shook her brother to the core. I foresaw what would happen next, and grabbed the waste bin as she vomited out what I knew to be the serpent and other evil spirits. Joshua was praying in the Spirit with fervour as I commanded every one of them to leave in Jesus' name.

Meanwhile, I learned later, the children were gathered in horror downstairs as they heard their well-controlled and sweet mother retching with such violence. As her sobs died down and she wiped the sweat from her brow she said,

'How can all that come out of me, a saved woman?'

I explained that this was the ignorance which abounded in the Church, alas, and why so many congregations worshipping in Spirit and in truth would nevertheless rapidly join any prayer line which formed in their assemblies. Joshua's sister hugged and kissed me, and looking into my eyes said,

'I've heard all about you, I have read your books and

now I have been exposed to your ministry. It is very clear that the Lord brought you here to set me free.'

No wonder the Father had said to me, 'Tell her I love her.'

Later on I explained to her three very handsome children why their mother was screaming and making such a noise. I explained it to the dear little girl and the two boys about eleven and fifteen. They all asked to be set free. I answered them that God had it all in hand, but the timing would be His.

The next day brought the arrival of Joshua's youngest sister to the house for a short stay. She was another delightful, handsome woman of God, with a deep love of Jesus that was evident in everything she said and did, bless her. Like Joshua's other sister, she blessed me. Those sisters were genuine in their faith. Jesus was real to them, and Lord in their lives.

On that same trip to Malaysia I had a lovely reunion with a Chinese sister, Mei Lee. I had kept in touch with her ever since my first trip to Penang ten years ago. She left Penang to work on the mainland eventually, but would always make the journey to the island to see me, bless her.

She was of a sweet and gentle nature and had been incredibly shy when I first met her. She was a lodger in the missionaries' house I was blessed to use, and I had such a liking for her.

She was also my first contact with a demon called 'Spirit of the Faceless One', a spirit which goes hand in hand with shy and ugly spirits. These people always feel of no account, totally unnoticed and rejected, even by the Body of Christ. They are almost apologetic for their existence, and so it was with Mei Lee.

She also had a skin problem which did not help. This was found to be due to rice and wheat. She followed the diet I gave her and got a lovely clear skin. A lot of people think that their skin problems are demonic when it is simply a genuine allergy.

I ministered to this precious sister who was transformed into a very lovely young woman. She remained grateful and I always felt her love. She was a constant chauffeuse, if I needed one, whenever I went to Penang until she left for the mainland.

I was delighted when I found she lived quite near the hotel where I was staying and we arranged to meet. Late one afternoon there was a tap on my door. I invited the caller in, making sure I recognised the voice. What a surprise I had. Such a radiance, such a joy!

I thought, 'She must be in love,' for I know that look well having ministered to so many women.

We embraced and shared the news up to date. She had something exciting to tell me. Yes, she was in love and about to marry a man younger than herself. It can be a problem for the Chinese but should not be for Christian Chinese.

In my experience, it can be felt a disgrace for a male Chinese to marry a lady older than himself. A man of eighty can have a bride of sixteen and that is alright, but a lady of eighty-two, definitely not! Alas, such ingrained prejudice can affect relationships as well in Christian Asians (or even Europeans, including British!) unless dealt with by the Holy Spirit.

Mei Lee had sat through many of my teaching ministries and certainly did not need deliverance. We prayed and broke bread together and she revealed that her fiancé had a problem, part of which was involvement with martial arts in order to defend himself from persecution in the Arab world where he worked. The other part was a curse.

At birth an astrological prognostication was made

over him that because of his birth date he would always clash with his father and they would never be compatible. So he was given away and brought up by a relative because he did indeed, as was the curse spoken over him, always clash with his father. Can you imagine the curse of rejection over that young man?

All this was dealt with in a ministry we arranged before their marriage at the end of January. Joshua stood with me and this very special young man, clearly an ideal husband-to-be, was mightily set free, praise the Lord!

They were both so grateful, and sent us a generous love offering. I really believe the Lord repaid this lovely sister, pressed down and running over, for the unconditional servanthood she had shown me from the first time I visited Penang, when she had felt she was a nobody.

God knew she was a somebody and indeed so it has proven. She is a child of God, joint heir with Christ, hallelujah! Bless them both in their new life together.

Chapter 13

Ministry to the Children

I knew I would not be staying too long at Joshua's sister's house and I needed to minister to the three children there, two handsome boys, one a teenager, one preteens, and a pretty little girl a bit younger.

Now I want to share something else that is very common in Hinduism. It is mesmerism. I believe that the Lord has shown me that due to ancestral worship of cobras, those from Hindu ancestry are subject to being mesmerised. That mesmerism includes that of being mesmerised by the television or cinema screen.

I have watched so many of this ancestry glued to the TV, watching rubbish, although they are Born Again and Spirit-filled. It is quite uncanny. The same could be said of Africans, but my experience with regard to them is not as long-term as it is for those of Hindu ancestry.

On many different occasions I observed each of those children, as I had Joshua, when watching TV. Their faces were not normal and tended to be trance-like. I would talk to them, even shout at them when they were watching garbage, but they certainly did not hear.

Moreover, in contrast to the sister's warmth, and the ability of the two younger children to hug and embrace me and each other, it seemed the elder boy for whom I felt a deep compassion, although I didn't know why, had a marked inability to embrace, hug or even bend in their direction when greeting people. To be honest, he was as stiff and unyielding as a board, totally bound!

I knew of course that the Hindu pride was there, but Joshua told me he was often sick, and he looked so dark and, as I said, bound, mesmerised and unable to show love or affection.

All three children had spirits of fear. With Joshua and his sister from Australia covering me, I started with the little girl, leading her through the freedom from curse prayer (see *Fruit Abiding in the Vine* Chapter 27: 'How to Come Out from Under the Curse'). I reassured the younger boy, who was being cuddled by his mother on the sofa and who started weeping and clinging to her.

I will not go into the ministry to the younger children, but praise God they were set free. For the purpose of teaching, and of course that is the purpose of all my books, I will detail the amazing events concerning the eldest son.

Following the freedom from curse prayer we could not seem to move on and get the evil spirits out. There was a block, a complete block to the ministry, yet I knew this young man wanted to get free. Actually I could see a great similarity in him to Joshua. I liked the respectful way they treated Joshua as their uncle.

I told those assembled to pray in the Holy Spirit whilst I waited on God to reveal by His Spirit what ailed the boy. Suddenly I got a vision. It was of a foetus shrivelled up in the womb. It wasn't dead, although barely alive. I also saw a powdered white head. I relayed what I had seen to those assembled and the mother started to weep very profusely. The story was this.

During the pregnancy with her first child, married to

a non-practising Hindu whom she married not being Born Again herself at the time, she lived with her mother-in-law who was a practising and devout Hindu lady. There were no problems between mother and daughter-in-law until she became pregnant, and then the mother-in-law became very nasty to her.

She wept as she told me that daily her mother-in-law returned from the temple with powder on her head, and she felt she had been cursing her unborn child. Since she was definitely a Christian by then, this would have been an affront to the mother-in-law, that maybe a child would be born and not brought up as a Hindu.

'My poor boy, my poor boy,' she wept.

I consoled her and explained that it could be that the unborn child **was** being cursed unto death, and that is certainly what I was getting. In the name of Jesus I proceeded to cut him off from the Angel of Death and commanded the spirit of death to leave. Nothing happened. The block continued, the child's almost black eyes stared listlessly ahead.

As readers will know I rarely address demons. However, after a considerable time trying to break through the powers of darkness enveloping him, I addressed the spirit, demanding to know its name. The reply came swiftly in one word,

'Hatred.'

I can tell you, readers, that hatred is a very, very strong and powerful Hindu spirit. It is, in fact, what we call a strong man. Knowing its name now, I commanded it to go in the name of Jesus, reminding it that it had no place or power in this young man through the blood of Jesus.

It left very quickly. Death and all its minions followed, and what an exciting time we all had! I smile and my heart leaps with joy as I recall what followed.

This precious young man was able to embrace and kiss his younger brother and sister and me, whom he had been really steering clear of, although he was extremely polite. He lifted me up in the air with pure joy! It was indeed a very happy ending for those children, and indeed their mother and aunty and uncle who stood with us.

We give God all the glory and declare that what He has begun in that family He will bring to completion for His Word's sake. All of the children were special, they had real potential. It is at such times one wants to stick around and see them walking in deliverance, quitting TV, etc. Alas we cannot do it all!

Following this ministry I had such a conviction in my spirit that since this lovely Christian family had not confessed and repented the idolatry of Hinduism, I really ought to minister to the mother, a widow, and also the elder brother, if possible. She was living several hours journey away and I knew I would soon be moving to a hotel, where both Joshua and I could rest and refresh ourselves before travelling together to see them.

The elder brother informed me that the mother never allowed anyone to minister to her. However, she had read my first two books, and I knew she was very grateful to me for assisting with Joshua's treatment in England, so I telephoned her and she was, in her own words, longing to meet me, and agreeable to whatever I thought was right.

I just want to mention here that whilst in that area I visited a local Church where Pastor Eu Hong Seng was teaching on Joshua. I not only enjoyed his teaching but his witty snippets. One of those was:

'The best thing to do behind a Christians's back is to pat it!'

Chapter 14

The Most Horrifying Ministry of my Life

In spite of the expectations of her eldest sons that she would not do so, Mamma agreed to ministry. She was indeed a simply lovely soul, but I spoke to her on the telephone of her need to be set free of ancestral spirits, and to repent the idolatry of Hinduism, however long she had been a Christian.

It meant a long journey and I was still quite tired, as indeed was Joshua who had also not been very well. The sister from Australia was to be returning to the family home and we were to take her with us. The journey would take three or four hours, but I would see a lot of Malaysian countryside en route. I looked forward to that, having been disappointed at paying so much for a car which was only used for shunting back and forth locally.

Joshua collected his youngest sister and we set off in the early morning. Like all Malaysian mornings it was extremely hot, with the promise of more intense heat, and birds singing their hearts out whilst they had the energy to do so. I was pleased to get into the air-conditioned car, and I was longing to meet Mamma.

When I did meet her, she was arrayed in a sari which she apparently always wore. I could see how beautiful she must have been as a young woman. She looked typically Indian to me, however much a Malaysian citizen she was!

She welcomed the three of us into the house together with two of Joshua's brothers. We had visited at the family business which employed some two hundred factory workers. There was the wife of the younger son, whose home it was, and two lovely children, obviously adored by Mamma who minded them whilst their mother worked, running around the house.

The house was new and very beautiful and palatial. Everything was colour-coded, from the beautiful silk carpets to the most exquisitely draped curtains. The floors appeared to be a sort of marble, the lighting was magnificent and they also had a European loo as well as the Eastern squatters type. The bathrooms were lovely, and everything was in excellent taste.

I learnt that the house had been built less than a year, and occupied only a few months. The garden was designed but not completed yet. Joshua had not seen this house before and found it quite luxurious. It spelled out to him that the family business was doing well, and that he had seemed to be cut out of his inheritance by his elder brother because of former heroin addiction. He was bitter about that at that time, but prayer resolved matters when forgiveness took place.

The time for ministry arrived. Joshua and his youngest sister were really the only two who knew what I was at. I explained carefully to Mamma what was to take place and how I would break the curses and call out the spirits executing the curses, following her prayer of confession and repentance of the sins of the forefathers, known and unknown, which included the idolatry of

Hinduism. She also had to forgive her father for cruelty to her mother, which she had not done before.

One brother and his wife stood to the side and the elder brother stood apart to the rear of Mamma. I was not at all happy about his presence and there was also a strong mocking spirit, a Hindu strong man I was confronting from him, but I silently bound that before commencing.

All the instructions to Mamma were given with great difficulty because some very strange things happened, which led to probably the most demanding warfare in ministry I have ever encountered. The sequence of events was as follows.

As I attempted to explain procedure, a roaring sound came over the house. It was like a wind, but wasn't a wind. The youngest sister said,

'It's like someone is very angry. It's anger.'

The roaring increased so that none of us could hear ourselves speak. I was almost shouting to raise my voice above the din. Then the beautiful curtains stood out literally horizontally from their curtain rods as the sound of the wind increased. But was it a wind?

Something crashed in the kitchen. I felt it had fallen off a wall. Someone went to investigate. Before they returned the windows started to rattle, and I felt as if the house was being crushed from the outside. Water started to pour in everywhere, including down the central light.

Suddenly I was paddling. I sensed terrible fear in all present.

'Don't flake out on me. Stand!' I said.

I could hear Joshua and two others praying in the Spirit. Mamma stood there confused and dumbfounded. Having assured myself that it was not a monsoon, that the house in any event had been through monsoons and not leaked, I knew it was a tough warfare.

Then the lights fused. The water was threatening silk carpets and drapes. Three persons went to fetch pails and mops.

During all this time I stood firmly in position, declaring Psalm 91, Psalm 46 and many Scriptures. *'Greater is He that is within me'* and *'The weapons of our warfare are not carnal but mighty in God,'* etc., etc. On and on I went until the din was unbearable, and the house was shaking.

'Stand. Keep standing,' I told everyone as I continued to confront the enemy.

How I thanked God for Joshua and his sister. I also looked up and saw a wall clock. On one side of it was a unicorn, the other side was a pegasus.

'That will have to go,' I thought.

Meanwhile, the lady whose beautiful home it was displayed such a fear I had to minister deliverance to her. I could hear all their thoughts!

'This woman we hardly know has come from England. Now our lovely house is being destroyed.'

I bound everything I could think to bind and I was quietly saying,

'What next, Holy Spirit?' when words from one of the few prophecies made over my life which I kept in my Bible came strongly to mind. The date of it was 27.9.91 and the part which is important is reproduced below.

'My Beloved Daughter, My heart is full and overflows towards you. I have watched you grow under My hand as a proud parent watches over a beloved child. I have sown many seeds of what you have done and I have sown yet further seeds of what you shall be able to accomplish in My name.

Beloved, you are as yet unaware of all that I have

for you to do. All this time it has been a training. I shall continue to train you and I will teach you more of the ways of my enemy that you may expose him more.

Do not be afraid, for you **shall** tread on snakes and scorpions and, Beloved, it does not matter how big they are. My Word is that they shall not harm you, therefore do not fear. Do not fear, no matter how big the adversary appears to be. Do not fear, no matter how loud he **roars** and shouts. Do not listen to his threats. Do not even countenance his lies.

Know that I am with you. I will uphold you within my righteous right hand. I will encompass you with my protection. I will undergird you with my everlasting arm.

Beloved, this is permanent. You will not be left alone for I have placed my **special** protection around you, and the angels assigned to you are **mighty**. They wield My sword in their hand. They shall wield it continually on your behalf. They shall minister to you accordingly, as you continue to walk with Me.

Your strength shall not fail. Your bones shall not weaken. Your heart shall not be overstretched. Your resources shall not run out. I will supply **all** that is needed in every way. Trust Me and rely on Me. Do not hesitate to draw from My well of resources, for it will **not** run out. It is infinite and everlasting. My resources will always be sufficient, yes, **more** than sufficient. And there shall be overflowing abundance as you continue, as My child, to pour out your abundance. There shall be an abundance of all good things for you, that you may bless Me and My people.

Beloved, My heart is full for you, for you are the delight of My heart. Receive My blessing. Receive My joy. Receive the seal of My approval. Receive My Word for your life. Enter afresh and continue to draw the oil from Me.'

Having let those words I knew almost by heart float through my brain, as it were, I snatched at: 1. The promise; 2. The description of the enemy; 3. The assistance available.

This was part of a prophecy from someone whose prophecies have been proven in a very powerful way, including two made over myself, otherwise I would not share them. It is necessary to do so because I needed all of that prophetic word. It was a mighty outpouring from Jehovah Jireh, and all the provision referred to I found to have been true three years after the prophecy was made.

So I would not fear the enemy, however loud he **roared**. By the time I had reached this stage of events I can only describe the noise as terrifying. I sensed those around in the most part had felt I was weakening, but I was listening as they prayed. I said,

'Father, your servant had said that the angels assigned to me are mighty. Will you please send them to assist me now and let them be over this house?'

Immediately the roaring ceased, the wind stilled, the waters stopped pouring in and that feeling of pressure from outside, squeezing the house, relaxed.

We then praised the Lord. I was so excited. The Father had sent the angels that I had asked for, and what I was confronting here was a very powerful stronghold of Hinduism, that was for sure.

By the way, please **never** give angels orders or command angels. Only the Father has that authority, and I could write a whole book on the disasters of commanding angels, which we do **not** have scriptural authority to do. Ask God to send His angels to assist, and if He is willing to He will do so. I have seen whole ministries virtually destroyed or damaged when folks commanded angels, including my own!

Many years ago I received an incorrect teaching on this subject and reversed what I had originally accepted as biblical, which was that we do **not** have authority to command angels. The result was that I got a very large and powerful 'angel of light', which almost wrecked what God had set up, and destroyed the team. All this had to be repented, of course.

This book is to expose as many dangers to the Body as possible in these End Times. One danger is the curse of trusting in man (Jeremiah 17:5). Only the Word is our handbook. No man, no teacher, no prophet, no pastor, nobody is absolutely infallible, and that includes me. Check out everything I give you with the Spirit of all truth. Seek holiness unto the Lord as the most precious asset for your spiritual walk.

Following the minsitry, the pegasus and unicorn were smashed. As we were leaving, Joshua and I both noticed that the downpour had been only over that house! There were no puddles in the road, or over the grounds of any other properties.

'That was for real,' I said quietly after a long silence on the way home, during which time I was seeking God.

'What was it, Holy Spirit?' I asked. Back came the reply like a rocket.

'The gods of air, fire and water.'

My mind reeled. What had I done ever since my arrival in Malaysia this time? I had been freeing Hindus from the gods of the air, fire and water; Hindus who had converted but not renounced these powers. Yes,

Christians whose spiritual walk had been blocked by those ancient and ancestral strongholds. I had been Jehovah Jireh's instrument for all this family, I believe because their Mother always prayed for all her children.

I tell you, since that time I have had a surging desire in my breast to pray against those curses, after repentance of every Christian with a Hindu background, right back through the blood line, to cleanse it absolutely of these demonic gods. Hallelujah, lead me there, Lord, let these yokes be broken in Jesus' holy name!

I also have to say this, and I say it with absolute conviction. The ministry to Mamma brought about an attack from Malaysia which has ruthlesly and relentlessly continued until now, as I write this book. I and my beloved team have been warring against foreign gods, believe me. What I would have done without these stalwarts, God alone knows.

I would like to mention here that insanity is another powerful Hindu demon. That has to be, when you consider those ancestors who would ritually slit their own throats, or castes who required wives to put themselves on their husbands' funeral pyres! What is more the wives would do it. Such things have to be insanity.

Hindus are also stoics. In their culture they do not register emotion, neither joy nor sorrow. The women are also downtrodden, regarded largely as servants and breeders of the blood line.

The mocking spirit is strong in both Hindus and Chinese who worship the dragon. Again, just as Hindus need the Kundalini cut, the astrological prognostications and idolatry repented, and to be cut off from every god of air, fire and water, the nether world and nature, so the Chinese need cutting off from the dragon, their false god. There will be more of this in my next book!

Chapter 15

Hotel Ministry

Well, we were both very tired when we arrived back at the hotel, and were so glad for the rest. We used to meet at the poolside after breakfast and I would do my Bible study and prayer time in the hot sun, which I desperately needed on my bones.

One blazing morning a young Chinese man, in his mid-thirties we guessed, came to the poolside and walked around it. The pool previously seemed to be shunned by all visitors, who were busy talking in the continuously open, large restaurant which overlooked the pool.

The young man gazed around the area which was scattered with white chairs and tables. Maybe he felt our eyes upon him, I don't know, but he walked uver and said,

'May I join you?'

We both sensed a great loneliness in him but also a fear. Our Bibles were obviously on the table, together with my copious notebooks. He asked,

'Are you Christians?'

We replied that we were and immediately got into witnessing. Joshua had such a good rapport with the Chinese that I sat back to listen to his witness.

This young man, whom I shall call Peter Yang-ho, was attending a conference at the hotel concerning the pharmaceutical industry he was involved with. He told us that it was his seventh and last week there. He would fly back to China in forty-eight hours.

We both felt very disappointed at that, and Joshua realised he should move fast. He gave his own testimony of twelve years heroin addiction in Pakistan and discovered that this young man had a matrimonial problem due to mother-in-law interference. He really loved his wife, but was suffering because of the Jezebel influence upon her from her mother. We discerned this and told him that our Father could also take care of that.

Joshua led him to the Lord in that beautiful simple way that always touched my heart, and Peter wept. I had several tracts to give him and a little booklet and Christian calendar with a Scripture for each day of the year. Heaven knows how many of those I gave away. I took fifty and only had about ten left at that point.

We exchanged addresses and I gave him copies of my first two books. He revealed to us that he actually owned a Bible someone had given him and we encouraged him to really get into the Word daily. He left for China a lot happier than he was before.

I should add that Peter ultimately visited England, and contacted me from a hotel where he was staying to say that he was really walking with the Lord. It was such a pity that although he left three mesages on my answerphone, he did not leave his contact number. When he finally got me at the Clinic he was just about to travel back to China. Never mind, we'll meet again, I am sure. Praise the Lord he felt to telephone and update us with such happy and encouraging news.

Meanwhile, I was feeling the hotel was really too expensive to remain there. So did Joshua, but we prayed about this because for some reason we both felt we should stay on. I loved all the melon, papaya, star fruits and kiwis I was living on. The hotel staff were very obliging in every way, and our heavenly Father was so good to us, meeting our needs in such circumstances with a special reduction in room prices!

His mercies were indeed new every morning at that hotel, even to the extent of intervening regarding a dreadful smell of mould along the corridor where our room was. When I investigated, with a handkerchief over my mouth and nostrils, I found a hideous breakdown in the plaster further along the corridor, and fungus was having a fair old time reproducing in that area.

I saw the management and gave them a potted history of Candidosis, pointing out that the spores could break loose and cause severe chest infection or respiratory problems, not only for visitors but for staff. I said that until they could gouge out the soaking wet affected area of the plaster, they could kill the spores with bleach. Amazingly, that's what they did, and I subsequently heard from an English-speaking Chinese waitress that many in the hotel suffered from repeated respiratory dysfunction of one sort or another.

This rather lovely Chinese waitress was someone else we witnessed to. She was a student biding time on vacation, and she touched our hearts during celebration of Chinese New Year with a gift of oranges and nuts. The gift was left outside my door and a note pushed underneath saying,

'You will never know how much I have been helped by talking to people like you.'

I had another interesting experience in the hotel forecourt during my stay. A hefty Australian came to the foyer counter as I was collecting my room key, en route from the poolside where I had been soaking up the sun.

He was with two children about twelve and fourteen years of age and changing some money.

I felt that he was giving me the eye and I found myself binding a lust of the eyes in Jesus' name. He sidled over and opened a conversation.

'Hi! You British?'

'Yes.'

'Staying here?'

'Yes, are those your children?' I enquired, trusting a wife and mother would shortly be on the scene.

I was very concerned with the boy, presumably his son, who was puffing a Ventolin inhaler strapped to his chest. The man offered me a cigarette. From the appearance of his nicotine-drenched countenance and stained fingers I could tell that he was a heavy smoker. Declining the proffered cigarette I said politely,

'No, thank you. I don't smoke, and neither should you, if that is your son struggling over there.'

The child had moved to a sofa in the forecourt which was heavily decorated for Chinese New Year celebrations.

'You are right,' the man responded, throwing his cigarette in the trash can. 'I keep trying to give it up. I am having heart surgery shortly and I'm scared to death.'

'Let's get this lot for Jesus,' I thought.

Slightly shifting my icy position I asked politely where he was from and was he on holiday? Where was his wife?

'She is at home having a baby.' He told me. 'I brought the kids here for a break. We're doing the lakes in half an hour's time with a picnic. Like to join us?'

'No, thank you, I am busy. Surely you should be close to your wife at such a time. I'd like to speak to you about your son.'

'Oh, it's not my baby,' he replied. 'My wife and I are divorced,' as though that made everything right!

I suggested we had a juice by the pool, if he didn't smoke. I told him how disgusting he smelled and that since his son clearly suffered severe asthma, he was exacerbating it by smoking in his presence. Here was a real man of the world. His face told its own story of the round of gin and tonic parties, sun worship, sex and gluttony.

I had put my arm around the little boy and we walked from the foyer to the pool. He was a dear little chap. I wanted to get down to business quickly, but before I could start his father pushed his business card across the table with his room number pencilled on it.

'This is my room number, if you are interested,' he said.

'I'm not,' I replied, and of course his interest in me waned rapidly.

The seducing spirit recoiled deep into his gut, doubtless to await its next possible prey. So first I put on my medical journalist's hat, and gave medical references on the carcinogenic affects of sidestream smoke, now proven beyond measure. He was agreeing with me, whilst wanting to push off quickly.

I then illustrated that the onset of asthma could often be fear, and quickly established that it was in Matthew's case. I further elaborated on the danger of him smoking up to the time of heart surgery, reminding him of his spoken out fear with regard to this.

He kept getting up to go, looking at his watch. Fear was in operation! He was hostile, so was his daughter who started to giggle and also wandered off.

The gospel was given quickly. How I wished Joshua was there! He was better at giving the gospel and the cross, and although I had learnt a lot from him he could still teach me a great deal.

Well, it was a definite resistance from the father and

107

the daughter, but I saw how interested Matthew was. The father got up, looking at his watch, and said,

'We must move, kids, or we'll miss the lakes.'

Looking him straight in the eyes I said,

'Look, I can see you're not receiving what I am saying, but Matthew is. Matthew, am I right?'

'Yes.' He nodded as he spoke.

'Give me ten minutes with Matthew alone,' I requested. 'I'll take him into the forecourt.'

The father agreed. Matthew was brought to salvation sitting beneath all the trappings of the hotel entrance decked for Chinese New Year. I then cast out a spirit of fear and infirmity. I believe he was healed by the power of the Lord Jesus and His name.

I quickly counselled him how to resist the enemy should an asthma attack come, and returned him, anointed with oil, to his agitated father. They disappeared in a cloud of smoke but I knew that Matthew was safe in the arms of Jesus.

In these ministries Jehovah Jireh had provided both for Peter and for Matthew, praise His name!

Chapter 16

The Vision of Frankie

I was praying in the Spirit in my hotel room before going down to the pool. I used to pray in the Spirit always as I opened my eyes each day, and would go on indefinitely until I took my daily communion, with a cracker and whatever juice I could lay my hands on.

Whilst praying I saw the head of a man with hair that looked like the large headress of an Indian Chief in the movies, not that I had seen one for twenty years! As I prayed I knew this was a person and that I had to minister to him or her. Was I going to meet a Red Indian in the hotel I wondered?

Anything could happen. There was a great stirring and bustle as the place got really heavily decked out for the Chinese New Year, with its dragon's heads and paraphernalia.

When I met Joshua at the pool I shared with him and he looked startled.

'Look,' I said, 'I'll draw what I saw and you tell me if it means anything to you.'

He looked at my sketch.

'Pearl,' he said, 'it's Frankie.'

'Frankie who?' I asked.

'Frankie my friend. He had hair he used to wear just like that. Ooh, Pearl, I must telephone him.'

'Well, watch the phone bill,' I said, 'because it's long distance.'

'OK, I'll be quick.'

He quickly got Frankie on the phone and I heard him say,

'Look, Frankie, Pearl has had this vision and when she gets these things it's of the Lord. You better come quickly. Here, you speak to Pearl.'

Just like Joshua, an economy of the spoken word as always! I loved the way he got everything completed in a couple of sentences. It was like the way he buttoned up people for the Lord!

I spoke to Frankie and convinced him he should come. Joshua said he would organise some accommodation for him which was being offered for special rates for Chinese New Year visitors.

When he went downstairs to organise a room in the travellers' quarters, a very basic unit of bed and shared bathroom, he said to the receptionist at the desk that surely we as visitors should also have the special terms applied to us. Praise God, the charges for our hotel rooms were reduced yet again for the rest of our stay! None of Joshua's family could believe it. We were now in a four star hotel for roadside bed and breakfast prices!

Frankie arrived. He was a slim, unpretentious young man, gentle and polite in nature. Clearly there was a strong soul tie between Joshua and Frankie due to their being partners in crime during their exploits in Pakistan as heroin addicts and pushers. At this point it was difficult to envisage them as parties to any such violence and evil.

Frankie and Joshua were to have breakfast together. I

was to join them at the poolside for coffee so they would have some time alone. Frankie, who had also been a martial arts exponent, had written to thank me for the help I had given Joshua, but I did not really know him except to hear of their exploits in Pakistan. He had said,

'I think you are God's provision for Joshua. He got to get it right this time, no more drugs, and fixed to do what God say him to do.'

When he arrived we all sat by the pool and I began quite spontaneously to minister to Frankie by the testimony of God's loving kindness to me, for a start, and of miracles I had witnessed. I related many situations where I had seen the miracle-working power of Jesus Christ and revelation of the Holy Spirit in so many entirely different areas, which illustrated clearly that Jesus is indeed Lord of every area of our lives if we allow Him to be.

As I spoke I noticed a very definite change in Frankie's demeanour. He started to tremble and to weep. I left my chair and went over to him. Placing my right hand on his left shoulder, I prayed in the Holy Spirit as his controlled weeping broke out into sobs which could not be checked.

'Let it all go, Frankie, the Lord loves you,' I told him.

Joshua was quite startled out of a dreamy stance and I said,

'Joshua, this is an encounter with the Holy Spirit. Come and pray with your friend.'

We both then prayed over Frankie in the Spirit and Joshua led him to the Lord. I could tell that it was a true conviction of the Lord Jesus received in his heart, and we all rejoiced. I gave him some Scriptures to read in a little book and some leaflets on the armour and the blood Scriptures, telling him to pray them every day.

He agreed that he should be baptised by immersion in

the pool following ministry for freedom of curse. We decided to invite a friend, Pastor Chang, to join us and his precious wife came also. There was so much fear to be dealt with, including a fear of water.

Frankie told us how when he was making the decision to come he could not sleep at all that night, and how a voice in his ears kept telling him not to book the seat on the train. Well, we all know who that was, but, praise God, we have the victory in Christ Jesus, hallelujah!

Pastor Chang and Joshua went into the pool either side of Frankie. I stayed on the side with my Bible, and on January 24th Frankie obeyed God's command to repent and be baptised.

> *'Then Peter said unto them, Repent, and be baptised every one of you in the name of Jesus Christ for the remission of sins, and ye shall receive the gift of the Holy Ghost.'* (Acts 2:38)

Frankie told us how in bed the night before his baptism he felt so afraid, and how he read the little booklet of Scriptures I had given him entitled *Pure Gold* and the fear left.

He was by trade a very brilliant gold and silversmith, as mentioned before. The business was his father's and in existence for thirty-four years. His brother who worked with him was also his partner, but unfortunately got caught up with a demonic lady with extravagant tastes and a liking for alcohol. He had started gambling and stealing the gold stored to make jewellery, and Frankie told us how serious the position was becoming. We prayed about that too and Frankie gave it to the Lord.

Exactly eleven months following his baptism I received a letter from Frankie and with his permission I give an exact extract from it, which touched the depths of my heart, for surely it illustrated that Frankie had indeed met with Jesus and grasped the gospel message.

'Now I sleep in a rented house nearly five months. My semi-detached bungalow with beautiful garden and badminton court given to bank waiting for public auction. From 16th October my father's thirty-six year old goldsmiths was closed, exactly within four years my elder brother brought (led) to ruin by gambling and drink. Of course he got marry a devil woman, illiterate, extravagant and alcoholic. Another defect is sunk in superstition, especially my elder brother in idolatry.

Thank God I am save and special thank to Joshua who bring me to Jesus love and baptism on 24th January 1993. Of course, Pearl's book *Go And Do Likewise* impress me, and influence me the most is Joshua's stories about Pearl and his own experiences.

Lord Jesus say "love your enemy." These words of God reminded me your incident occurred while you are applying visa to stay in the UK and the Word proven is true and right. I believe the Word of God and I practise it in my life. That's how I forgive my elder brother and his wife without any anger but peace and calm in my mind.'

Frankie was referring to Joshua applying for a visa to re-enter England. I had accompanied him to the Britsh High Commission as he had had such difficulty before. When we arrived at the High Commission Joshua was distinctly nervous when he saw an official there who had interviewed him before and would not grant a visa. What is more, he applied persecution tactics. Joshua had called out in dismay on seeing him again, and I simply told him to bless the man.

'Bless you, sir, bless you,' I said, and Joshua joined in.

The man went away, we never saw him again and Joshua got a permit to enter Britain again without any further problems.

When I received Frankie's letter I wept over it, and how I know deep in my heart that dear Frankie has found a greater treasure, Jesus, that Pearl of Great Price. As I read his letter I recalled the old Anglican hymn:

'Take my silver, take my gold
Nothing, Lord, will I withhold.'

I recall, as a then member of the Anglican Church when funds were being raised for an extension to house a bookshop as a bridge into the High Street, Hounslow, this hymn being played during collection time. I was at that time a newly deserted wife in a desperate financial state and I heard the Lord say,

'Give.'

I told Him that I had no silver or gold and He told me to look at my fingers. On my finger was a beautiful ring with ten perfectly matched Brazilian diamonds mounted on an intricate pierced-out gallery of gold and platinum. Two more diamonds were set in leaves to make the shoulders. It was a unique ring, designed by myself and made by my late Uncle Ray, a very clever gold and silversmith. I had been very proud to flash that ring on my finger at the age of twenty-two, I can tell you.

I got home from the service with that ring weighing heavily on my finger, and took it back to the Church to be sold for the bookshop fund. As readers will know, I have had to give much that was precious away but I have always received a double portion of blessing for obedience. One cannot out-give God, and He has shown Frankie so clearly that revenge is not sweet, especially for Christians!

> 'Dearly beloved, avenge not yourselves, but rather give place unto wrath: for it is written, Vengeance is mine; I will repay, saith the Lord. Therefore if thine enemy hunger, feed him; if he thirst, give him drink: for in so doing thou shalt heap coals of fire on his head. Be not overcome of evil, but overcome evil with good.'
> (Romans 12:19–21)

> 'If thine enemy be hungry, give him bread to eat; and if he be thirsty, give him water to drink: For thou shalt heap coals of fire upon his head, and the Lord shall reward thee.'
> (Proverbs 25:21–22)

Frankie Lai Chan Fai has given me permission to use his name. He understands what it means to overcome by the blood of the lamb and the word of his testimony (Revelation 12:11). I give his name here too for another reason.

I believe he is special and has shown incredible faith for one so new in Christ. All his correspondence speaks of Jesus. Please, will you rise up and pray for him, as the Lord leads you? He needs faithful intercessors and I know this will speak to some of you. Praise the Lord, He is Frankie's Jehovah Jireh.

Chapter 17

Chinese Dragon and Martial Arts

Just as those with Hindu ancestors have to be cut free from the gods of air, fire, water, the nether world and nature, so the Chinese have to be cut free from the Dragon.

This can be a life-changing event. I recall a lovely Chinese sister who, in spite of being Born Again for over twenty years, could not pray in the Holy Spirit nor raise her hands in worship and dance. Set free of the Dragon she was able to do all these with pure delight.

I have had carbon copies of such ministries here and abroad. I recall one young man who was very anointed but manifested fear each time we sat down together or with a group. I asked him if 'medicine man' meant anything to him. He said his unsaved father was a medicine man and had given him potions in the distant past as a child. All this had to be dealt with. He was then set free of the Dragon. Fear departed. So many Asians are given potions from 'medicine men' and all this must be dealt with.

Many are dedicated in temples as babies, some are given blood to drink. This has horrific effects which can include a real thirst for consuming bloody meat. Another Malay custom is to slit a cockerel's throat, drip the blood into a pan, fry and eat it. This disgusting habit causes horrific results. In Pakistan Joshua ate meat for years which was sacrificed to idols. The Bible is very clear on warning against this.

> 'But that we write unto them, that they abstain from pollutions of idols, and from fornication, and from things strangled, and from blood.' (Acts 15:20)

I have seen those who have consumed such meat, although Born Again, behaving with the anticipation of Molech about to be fed a live child as meat is dished up and eating it like a wild animal. Believe me, these things are true, and I'm not very popular with Satan for discerning them. Such eating of meat also causes tremendous lethargy, and if you watch the big wildcats after the kill of meat they are incredibly sleepy for hours, even days.

Chinese children, and indeed Malay or Indian children, in Asian areas where Chinese Dragon festivals take place will not infrequently join the throng of the processions. They get extremeiy contaminated although it may only be done in childish excitement.

It's like when John Linden-Cook used to describe how his dog would go out and make a row in his garden when she saw a hedgehog. The dog obviously couldn't touch the hedgehog because of its bristles, but was sniffing around it. When his dog came indoors she had to be de-flead because she was contaminated. So it is with the occult, it may only take one unsuspecting sniff for a transference of spirits to take place.

Similarly, people are contaminated by Martial Arts, men and women. In Asian countries, just as our children will skip or play hop-scotch on the paving or in the streets, so children even at the early age of four start martial arts, Karate, T'ai Chi, etc. It begins for fun, innocently. Then you find someone better than you and want to practise with them. This leads to such practices being second nature.

The next thing is that these teenagers are looking to a guru or master, to whom they have to bow. The moment such idolatry begins they are taken over. I've seen things as I can hardly relate, where totally responsible Christians have these demonic setbacks through former involvement in martial arts. In the violence, anger and hatred that is worked up in those who practise martial arts damage can be done to property and persons which later the guilty party simply cannot recall. That is because they are taken over.

I have lost count of those I have counselled with children or family members formerly involved in martial arts and, believe me, it can be terrifying if you do not know Jesus. If such an explosion happens in your presence, if you are attacked or intimidated by such an outburst say this:

'Be bound and go down, in Jesus' name.'

I will tell you, it works. It was a tip given me by John Linden-Cook who has had some horrific experiences in dealing with casualties of martial arts.

There is also a definite link between martial arts and drug-taking. The root spirit is always a demon of fear. Addicts are controlled by the fear of when they will get their next fix. The martial arts proficiency puts them in a position to extract drugs by threats, intimidation or actual violence.

Incidentally, on April 3rd 1993 I was teaching and ministering at Edgware for Foreward in Faith Ministries by the kind invitation of Pastor Joshua Samasuwo (not related to Joshua). The Lord caused me at the end to make an altar call for those involved in martial arts.

119

He has never done that before. The spectacular response was quite astonishing. Also amazing was the number of sweet, gentle-looking ladies who came up, many of whom had commenced their interest by being taught Judo for self-defence.

Another very unusual occurrence at that meeting was the outrageous and noisy interruptions of a former spiritualist medium, in whom the spirits hostile to my teaching of the Word of God were manifesting. She left the hall, cursing and swearing in the most foul manner, no less than seven times, but finally returned to be set free in Jesus' name!

Many remarked later on my cool as I continued, blessing her in Jesus' name but unaffected by her antics, to deliver that Word. All praise to Jehovah Jireh, who had provided me with a warning beforehand through an intercessor that some form of interruption would happen! This lady was also an actress and had broadcast on numerology, clairvoyance and so on. I quickly decommissioned and annulled every word she had ever spoken on the air!

I should say that the Lord caused me to have a professional video of that teaching on healing, deliverance and freedom from curse. When He spoke to me about that I told Him that I had not the money. A few enquiries made it seem financially impossible. However, two unexpected sums of money arrived totalling exactly what was needed in outlay and, believe me, those videos have blessed hundreds in prayer groups, solitary closets and all manner of gatherings, even hospices and the Salvation Army! Praise God for Jehovah Jireh!

If you require the set of three they are £34.50 plus £5 recorded post and packing from Christian Clinic for Environmental Medicine, Lane End, Highlands Lane, Westfield, Woking, Surrey, GU22 9PU.

Chapter 18

Testimony of Esther's Healing of ME

Well, let's have a little light relief from all that heavy stuff!

I have continued with great joy and blessing to fellowship with Sozo Ministries. Blessing after blessing has come for me and for all those I have sent to Sozo for love, fellowship, healing and an unforgettable encounter with the Holy Spirit.

I think what really delights me in that holy place is to see so many mighty men of God being raised up. In any Church I have attended for any number of years I have not seen this. I'm sorry to say so, but it is true. Marion Daniel has been my Pastor over two years. It is the most complete pastoring I have ever received.

I met Esther at Pastor Marion's house. She was a radiant teenager with a deep and fervent love of the Lord Jesus. He was clearly her all. This precious handmaiden of the Lord spent two years in the dark with ice packs scarring her forehead, and footdrop because of her feet being downward all that time. It was medically predicted that her eyesight would be permanently damaged. I asked her to write her testimony as a tribute to the loving God we serve.

Esther's Testimony, December 1993

'I became ill when I was 13 years old. The illness started with headaches, weakness and other flu symptoms. After five months of continuously getting worse a doctor diagnosed me with ME. I got so ill I couldn't sit up or feed myself.

I was taken to hospital for a second time after I'd been ill eight months. Going into hospital was a terrible experience, as most of the medical profession we encountered had very little understanding of ME, and very little sensitivity. I couldn't have visitors because they totally exhausted me for a long time afterwards. I am blessed with a wonderful Mum who looked after me full time.

My eyes were very sensitive to light so I had to lie in a dark room (like having a migraine). The illness kept me bed-bound so I was robbed of all life I should have had. I am so thankful to God that during all this time the Lord Jesus kept me hanging on. His presence was continuously with me. I realised after many efforts by the medical profession to get me well that God was the only One who could treat me and I knew He would heal me.

The Lord lead my Mum into contact with some Christians who had been healed from ME. We found that there were lots of people in the country who had received miracles in the mighty name of Jesus through the ministry of Marion Daniel and Sozo Ministries. One of the ladies who had been healed sent me her testimony on tape. I listened to it a little bit at a time (because my concentration extended only to about one minute).

What she said was wonderful. She'd seen God's power. He had healed her, and her husband was saved, all in one week on a Sozo Conference. This was the kind of life-changing experience I'd been believing for. My parents who were both seeking God for my healing, got in contact with another married couple from Yorkshire. The lady had been miraculously healed from ME. They put us in contact with Marion Daniel. My Mum phoned Marion who spoke with such faith and told Mum,

"We can help your daughter."

The people from Sozo strongly advised my Mum to get me to listen to Scripture on tape even if it was so quiet I couldn't hear it. This is because in Proverbs 4:20–21 God says:

"My son, attend to my words; incline thine ear unto my sayings. Let them not depart from thine eyes: keep them in the midst of thine heart."

I started to listen to God's Word the same way I would take medicine. My faith grew as I heard about the ministy of Jesus and the fact that He healed all who came to Him for healing.

My parents were told about a Sozo Conference in a holiday village in Devon. A special man whose wife had a miracle said if I went I would come back sitting up. My Mum told me about all of this and after an initial refusal I yielded to God's plans, scarey as they were.

Friends lent my parents their Renault Espace car and a trailer. I lay flat on a mattress in the back of the car with the back totally blacked out. The trailer was full of all the things my Mum would need to look after me. We arrived on a Sunday afternoon in September after travelling 200 miles. It was a miracle that I was not as ill as I should have been after that long journey. For the last two years, with the exception of a visit to hospital, I hadn't been further than being carried down the corridor.

Mum met lots of healed people who spoke with so much faith. They believed I was going to be healed. On the Monday morning Marion and another minister prayed with me. God had given Marion amazingly accurate discernment and she knew exactly how God was going to set me free. This is when my healing began. Before the meeting my Mum was feeding me. I just knew that God wanted me to do it, so I rebuked the Devil in Jesus' name and fed myself. The strength came when I said the name "Jesus".

I was pushed to the meeting lying flat on a stretcher. Before we had got to the door I could feel the power of the Holy Ghost. All the people were praising God and giving everything they'd got to praising Him. They sang like I'd never heard people sing before. They clapped and Mum told me they were dancing (I had my eyes covered from the bright light). Marion preached, then prayed for me before I was pushed back to bed.

On Tuesday morning Marion prayed with me again. That dinner time I asked my Mum and the lady whose testimony I had heard on tape to help me sit up. I rebuked the Devil and quoted Scripture and sat on the edge of the bed. You have to know at this point that the doctor told my parents I would not be able to sit up immediately because of the blood rushing to my head. He also said that I would have drop-foot. My ankles wouldn't work properly because my feet were always flopped forwards. He said my eyesight would be permanently damaged because of the darkness. Everything I saw was yellow. When I sat on the edge of that bed in Jesus' name I had no pain, no pressure in my head, **no** dizziness. What I did have was strength.

On the Tuesday night meeting I heard every word of Marion's sermon. One thing she said particularly spoke to me. She said the Devil will do anything to stop you praising because it is such a powerful weapon against him. I thought,

"Right, I'm not going to let him do that any more."

When the music started I began to praise. We sang "For God is good, His mercy endures forever". Instead of my lungs getting painful and exhausted they got stronger and stronger. I began to quietly clap and as I did new life and strength filled my wrist and arm muscles. I danced in praise by moving my feet, and strength poured into all the muscles I used.

After the meeting I was pushed back to our chalet. I lay in bed waiting to sleep but praise began to well up in my heart. I sang, then clapped, then moved my feet. It was so exciting. I turned on my back, waved my arms in the air, then my legs. New life and strength filled every muscle.

My Mum came into the room and I asked her to put the main light on. When she did I looked straight at the bulb and had no pain in my eyes or head from the light. I danced in bed with my parents dancing with me until the early hours of Wednesday morning.

On Wednesday after more prayer I was pushed through to sit in broad daylight in the lounge. I looked out through the window at the beautiful crest and sky I had not seen for two years. Thursday was the last evening meeting. By then I could smile at the people at the Conference I had met and I sat on the front row.

After the preaching Marion said if there were people who wanted to go into deeper prayer with God they were to stand up. I felt like someone squeezed my stomach and I knew that was me! My Mum and a few other people helped me to my feet and held me up. When I put weight on my feet the pain was excruciating. I yelled out in Jesus' name, rebuking the pain and it went.

Then Marion, standing in front of me, beckoned me forwards. Shouting at the pain and weakness in Jesus' mighty name, I walked across the meeting room, about 16 metres. I then led the worship and prayed down the microphone. The people at the Conference were wonderful. They prayed for us and believed for my healing and gave us a lot of support.

On Friday in the name of Jesus I sat outside in the brilliant sunshine. We prayed by the swimming pool. It was a miracle I could concentrate on everything they said at the same time as I was taking in all the activity of children around the pool. My parents and I had lunch by the pool.

That afternoon I was baptised in the swimming pool and I actually bore all of my own weight in the water. The feeling was wonderful. That evening everyone on the Conference went out for a meal at a golf club. There God set me free to eat sugar again, which I hadn't done for a long time.

Since then I have not had any relapses at all, and I have perfect vision. The doctor had told me I would have scars on my forehead, from the severe burns caused by the ice packs to relieve the headaches. The sore patches, which were sometimes big scabs, went during the week and by the end of the Conference there were no scars at all.

Glory to God! I jog, dance, swim and drive, living life in all its fullness (John 10:10). I am making up for lost time in exams at college. God is faithful to His Word. What He says in His Word He is able also to perform (Romans 4:20).'

In every instance in this testimony we see Jehovah Jireh making provision for Esther.

Chapter 19

Miracle-Working God

Tony and Doreen

Another blessing of Jehovah Jireh is clearly illustrated by this testimony. In 1993 a beautiful couple visited the Clinic. It was very unusual for me to open the door but every one of the staff was occupied and I was passing through the hallway. I opened the door and was greeted by the words of these total strangers,

'We love you, Pearl.'

It was the beginning of a special friendship. Doreen and Tony were, like so many, brought to the Clinic by divine intervention. Their arrival certainly illustrated for me a gift that I had no idea I possessed, to minister and counsel in marriage and divorce cases as led by the Holy Spirit, the One True Counsellor.

This was another personal confirmation of a prophecy brought to me in 1992 at Vision Bible School, Kuala Lumpur. It was to be the first of many such ministry and counselling experiences, and I suppose upon reflection I have had plenty of training in the field, praise the Lord!

'Christian' counselling using such things as inner healing and visualisation have been confirmed as occult techniques. Instead, I was given by an intercessor to pray according to Isaiah 11:2–4, asking for the Holy Spirit and counsel of wisdom and might and understanding.

Tony was as plump as his sweet wife was thin. She had written a desperate letter to me which arrived in a pile of so many that arrive weekly. Doreen had been coughing virtually non-stop for thirty years, and I do mean virtually non-stop. She was exhausted, and clearly this precious man was exhausted and irritated by this continual disturbing background for everything they did, social, domestic, etc, etc.

I recall vividly extracting Doreen's lamentation, beginning at the first verse, and scrawling a hasty reply to the poor lady.

'Get here quickly. You have Candidosis.'

I did not even wait to get it typed. Had I done so she would probably still be waiting! To make things worse they were newly-weds who had emerged from very devastating and horrific backgrounds. To put it mildly, in spite of their obvious brave overcoming I felt that deep inside they were both bleeding to death.

It was certainly no coincidence that when the absolute devastation, betrayal and treachery of their first marriages ended, the Lord in His great mercy put these two dear ones in little dwelling places with their gardens as near back to side as could be. It was the Father's rescue operation of binding together two desperately hurt people. But Doreen's perpetual coughing almost drove Tony to his coffin (excuse the pun)!

Doreen's history as a child was horrific and it is best told in her own words.

Doreen's History

'My childhood was that of a normal child in a normal happy home. My father was a printer and my

Mother was loving and caring. But when I reached the age of nine my Mother became very ill with cancer and finally died after two years of suffering. My father was devastated and soon found it too much for him, having to earn a living and running a home, plus trying to bring up a little girl.

In desperation he sold his bungalow in Oxford and tried to place me in a Dr Barnardos Home where I would be given love and care, but as I was not an orphan they could not take me in. So began my unhappy childhood as I spent three terrible long years being sent from one place to another (mostly family homes). I just could not settle and was very unhappy not being able to have a home of my own with a mother to hug and love me.

Even at school I could not find happiness for just as I began to form relationships with the other children I was moved on to yet another home, and therefore another school, until I had attended 13 schools, unsettling my education. Wherever I went, never could I find happiness. I so longed to be loved. Instead I felt that nobody wanted me. Rejected and desperate, I was sent to my Mother's sister's house. Little did I know what drudgery and mental cruelty I was to endure in this home, always filled with lodgers and paying guests.

It soon became a life of strict discipline. There was always so much work to do. Every night there was a large bucket of potatoes to peel. Then there was the kitchen floor to scrub, and if Aunty was not satisfied with the hard work that I had just carried out then I was made to do it again and again until she was absolutely satisfied that it was perfect.

In the morning I had to light all the fires after cleaning the ashes and grates. Then there were the lodgers' socks to darn, buttons to sew on shirts, not forgetting the many pairs of shoes to polish and finally, to scrub the kitchen floor again before going to school. Food was never plentiful as I was fed on left-overs, such as bacon rind cut from the lodgers' bacon to make my sandwiches.

If I had not scrubbed the kitchen floor in the morning this chore had to be accomplished during the school dinner time, which meant that there would be no time for me to have my dinner. Although she was a very wealthy woman she was also very mean. All I seemed to be doing was cleaning cupboards and scrubbing floors. On some occasions I had to scrub the garage floor and the drive. To aggravate my unhappiness I was never allowed to bring any friends home or even invite anyone for my birthday.

I did not dare to tell my father as I was terrified of what my Aunty might do, as she did not need much excuse to use the dog strap across my back when I rebelled against her. Only my half-brother Ron really knew what I was going through. My wardrobe was mostly second-hand clothes from the market, or garments discarded from my Aunty's friends that I had to alter myself to make them fit. They were awful as, no matter how I tried, these old ladies' dresses could not reflect the fashion as worn by my school friends.

Although my uncle stuck up for me at times, he disturbed me by sexually abusing me, and wanting to give me body washes as an excuse for fondling my body. I wanted to die. I could not see a way out or find happiness. Many times I tried to run away but there was nowhere to go. (I could never tell my father, even until the day he died in 1992.)

I was now 13, when one day my father came to fetch me for a weekend in Oxford to stay with what turned out to be some beautiful Christian friends. On Sunday we went to a Pentecostal Church service and I loved every minute of it, but I had to go back to my Aunty's. I was so depressed I felt that I just could not stand any more of this torment.

At last I was to live at Oxford with a Christian family. I was now 14 and a very shy and timid girl, weighing only five stone. I was very ashamed of my very skinny body. The church that this family attended was wonderful and Spirit-filled. After a few months I came to know my Lord Jesus whilst in bed, and eventually I was baptised in water and the Holy Spirit. It was wonderful to know that at last somebody really cared about me, but most of all loved me.

I was married at twenty years of age and had two lovely daughters. We were a very happy family, but after nineteen years of marriage my lovely husband left me for another woman. I was devastated and desperately unhappy once more. I remembered my wretched childhood and I was desperate to give my two lovely daughters all the happiness and security that I did not have when I was a young girl.

It was a desperate struggle to cope. I even attempted suicide, but this time of unhappiness was different as I now had the Lord to turn to. His love for me was so wonderful, for time after time He supplied my every need, and those needs were many. I could almost write a book about those years of struggle. I was alone with my lovely girls for nine years. Although the wounds had mostly healed the scars were still there and I found it very hard to imagine that I could ever trust a man again and lived only for my Lord Jesus and my girls.

But I missed the support and love of a man and began to pray for someone to come into my life. I was very clear with my prayers and laid down many conditions such as: he must love me for what I am, have no children, he must love my girls, but most important he must be a Christian, and a man of authority.

I had just moved into a new house that the Lord had provided for me and it was there I met my second husband, Tony, and that is yet another wonderful story. The only problem was that for thirty years I suffered from a cough which grew worse and worse. I did not know what caused it, whether it was stress or allergies, demonic or physical. Also I hardly ever slept properly.'

Now let us move to Tony's background, also given in his own words:

Tony's Hurt

'Although I may appear to be a strong and powerful man, I have one weakness, the need to live under the wings of love.

I was brought up in a lovely atmosphere of love that came from my parents who were strong believers in the love command of Jesus, to love each other and to treat every one as you would like to be treated yourself. I had been married for over fourteen years and my love for my wife was very deep.

Although we had no children of our own she took an active part in my Church and youth work and the young people became our family. Our home was an open house. Throughout the week we would have much fellowship and prayer meetings. God had blessed us with good jobs. My wife was a catering officer over several hospitals and I was a Senior Research Technologist working for British Leyland.

Our home was a beautiful bungalow built by the hands of her father high on top of a hill next to my in-laws home, which was given to us in a blessed way due to the death of my wife's grandmother. Her grandfather asked if her mother and father would live with him. This left the problem of the bungalow that her father had built. It was suggested by her parents that we purchase the bungalow but I could never afford the money required to cover the purchase since we were struggling with our own mortgage for our little house in Oxford.

It was finally suggested that we could rent the bungalow to help pay off the small mortgage on it, and upon the death of the grandfather either the bungalow or the grandfather's house would become ours. We finally agreed over a family hand shake. Nothing was settled with a solicitor (my first big mistake), for he was a lay preacher and a respected Christian in the Methodist community.

My life at that time was very full and I spent a great deal of time going about the Lord's work amongst the young people so much in need of God's message of love. Indeed, the little village chapel was so full of young people that they almost ran the Church, as they took up many of the duties of service to that Church. Life was exciting and fulfilling.

All was well. I was very happy and blessed in every way, until a man came onto the scene who was supposed to be dying of lung cancer. He needed to hear of God's heavenly kingdom, but as things turned out that was the very last thing on his mind as all he wanted was my wife. Slowly he gained my friendship by making himself very useful around the home and helping with the maintenance of our cars and boat.

As a man of trust and love for my wife I took her explanation as truth that her work was getting her down when her love for me began to become secondary. She began to miss some of the prayer meetings in our house on the pretext that she was ministering to this man who was supposed to be in crisis. My job was in danger due to cut-backs in research so my thoughts were divided thinly, with all the other day-to-day problems concerning the running of a large youth organisation, plus the more important problems of those young folk that God had given me the gift of counselling.

It came as a bolt out of the blue when I was made redundant. I was just not prepared for all the difficulties of finding new employment in a time of recession. Within only a few months my wife left me, and she seemed to disappear altogether after leaving a brief telephone message,

"It's me, I'm leaving you and I am not coming back."

I did not even have the chance to say goodbye.

I was reeling in shock. Just as Job had suffered, so did I. My in-laws suddenly would not talk with me any longer. What was going on? Then after only two days came the two letters from the same solicitors, one for divorce, the other from my father-in-law demanding that I leave the bungalow. I could not believe this nightmare that was taking place. I was to discover that my lovely wife had betrayed me months before, as slowly the truth began to come from many of our friends. Sadly we had a joint account which she and her friend really emptied under my nose.

My Church heard many rumours started by my wife of how I had mistreated her and carried out acts of unnatural sex. I was devastated and even more hurt to think that so many old Church friends actually believed this story. I was manoeuvred out of my Church offices, my hard work amongst the youth collapsed. I have heard since that I was dealing with the 'accuser of the brethren'. Sad to say, I knew absolutely nothing about demons until I met Pearl Coleman.

I prayed so hard to my Father God and asked Him to save me from this evil thing that had come upon me but nothing happened. I felt quite alone. As solicitors fought to and fro, my beloved wife visited her parents openly next door with her man. It hurt me so much to see the truth of this situation. They even stole my cat, the only thing left to cuddle! Out of one hundred and fifty job applications I had only one reply and that was negative.

I pleaded with God "what have I done to displease you, Lord?" but no answer came from the Almighty. Later that day I saw my father-in-law sobbing in his shed across the garden. Had he discovered the truth and was in repentance? I did not have the will or the strength to go over to him and ask, so I prayed for him on my knees that the Lord would comfort him and bless him.

Swamped with grief, I knew now what the name Judas meant and as the bills and demands mounted I knew that my time of strength had come to its end. I started to plan my accidental death. It was then that the Lord acted, but not in the way I could ever have imagined.

I made four, real, planned attempts on my life.

Attempt 1. As I was preparing to connect the wiring to my wrists, ready for my electrocution, the door bell rang. I thought "what an inconvenient time to bother me, just as I was trying to end my pain." It was my sister Daphne who felt she had to call in to see how I was. I did not tell her at that time what I was about to do.

Attempt 2. I went to the top of a nearby multi-story car park. There was no one around. I sat in tears on the edge of the parapet, when out of nowhere two powerful arms grabbed me from behind with a firm voice: 'It's not worth it, mate.' The courting couple had spotted me just in time from their car!

Attempt 3. Now I would use all my engineering ingenuity and succeed this time. I tried to set fire to my cabin cruiser with me inside it, only to be stopped by the crew of the ELCICA as it passed by. I was boarded by the crew who said, "We smelt petrol way back down stream. Looks like your fuel line has come undone. We'll fix it for you," and then departed back to the ELCICA. Later when I came to my senses and tried to contact the crew of the ELCICA, Thames Water, with whom every power boat must be registered, carried no record of a craft carrying this name! Yet I saw the boat, its name and the crew so clearly.

Attempt 4. At a speed of 98 mph I knew that if I hit a strong tree it would be over in seconds. I found the right road with the right tree. I was but yards away from the end when two little children riding their bikes came across my path. I made the most spectacular emergency stop of my life only three feet from the tree. I ran back to the field gateway that the children had made their escape through but there was no sign of them, not even tyre marks from their bikes, no clue whatsoever.

I fell to my knees in prayer, asking the Lord to forgive me for my lack of faith and my lack of understanding of how much He loved me and that He had a purpose for my life. He wanted me to live. From that last attempt the devil lost his power over my broken heart and mind, for my loving God was covering me with angels all the time and I had not noticed. I chose to live.

What happened after that can only be called divine intervention and over the last few years the Lord has replaced what the locust had taken away. I am no longer financially a rich man but I have gained new riches that no man can rob or steal, and a love for those who have trodden the path of pain and sorrow, for they are the greatest of all my brothers and sisters.'

Both Doreen and Tony married with great expectation for a new life. However, there was no way now that Doreen could cover up the desperate coughing fits which overtook her. Tony had secured a low-paid job to keep things going. It was a job much competed for and he needed to be anything but tired. I will let Doreen explain what happened because of her cough.

At My Wit's End

'For just over thirty years I have been suffering with a continuous cough that persisted both day and night. At times it got so bad it caused me to vomit and bring all my food up. I also suffered bad migraines which in turn caused me to be listless and irritable. I became so lethargic and fatigued both my new husband and I thought that I was going to die. Sleep evaded me at every turn.

Never having any energy I found it very difficult to work three days a week at the office. By midday all I seemed to want to do was to lie down and go to sleep. In fact on one occasion I was caught snoring in my office chair, which was very embarrassing, although the girls were very understanding about it because they knew of my predicament. As a Christian I really prayed to the Lord so many times to heal me. I was also ministered to through people with healing ministries but still I never seemed to get healed. I was beginning to become angry with God. I cried to my Lord so many times even out of sheer desperation,

"Lord, please do something for me or show me if I am doing something wrong that needs to be put right."

One day I came home from work and found a package that had been pushed through my front door. On opening it I found three books written by a "Pearl Coleman". They were sent to me by a lady I had not met whom apparently had been treated by Pearl at her Clinic.

To begin with I was very sceptical about what I was reading. I thought that many of the things that Pearl wrote about were ridiculous, especially the spirits and homoeopathy, as I wanted to see a homoeopath. Somehow I ended up with a visit to a herbalist which did not really help. Pearl was writing that homoeopathy was occult. I did not really believe that, but did I? There was so much I read which stirred my spirit.

As I read Pearl's words I felt God was really speaking to me in my spirit about so much, especially on the subject of forgiveness. At that time I was hurting in so many areas from people I had loved but who had caused me great sorrow. At one time I wanted to kill the woman who took away my first husband but God really dealt with me on that subject.

I just had to really repent, and mean it. For me it was not easy but God was so gracious with His love and patience that He gently encouraged me to both repent and forgive those who had hurt me so much. But as I carried on reading the book in bed I began to realize that I had a lot of forgiving still to do. It was then God spoke to me with the words,

"As you forgive others I will forgive you."

It happened just then in my bed, and I placed it all before God. A beautiful release came into my spirit that night. I now proceeded to read all three books one after the other, as they moved my spirit into a new path with God. At the back of her book I read the words,

"If we can help you either physically or spiritually, or both, please do not hesitate to contact us. Should you require the Clinic papers please send a stamped envelope."

It took me about two weeks to pluck up the courage to write to her about my cough. To my surprise she wrote back to me within two days stating,

"Pray about becoming a patient. You clearly have an allergy."

Two weeks later I plucked up courage to phone her to make an appointment (I was very nervous). I had no idea that I was about to meet a very incredible woman of God. I shall never forget my first appointment, July 13th 1993. I walked towards the front door of the Clinic with my husband, Tony. All the nerves were gone as we were warmly welcomed into her lovely home.

As we sat in the waiting room we both felt a strong presence of the Lord that filled us with awe and peace. This was holy ground. It was in this situation that we met two of Pearl's staff Ruth and Henrietta, who took down searching notes of both my medical and personal details. On meeting Pearl I was made to feel so relaxed by the love that she radiated towards me.

I was thoroughly tested for two hours and was told that I was suffering from such a severe Candidosis condition that Pearl was amazed I was still able to walk about. I had so many food allergies like sugar, grains, dairy products and many more. But, oh, I loved my doughnuts! When I went shopping in my dinner hour in Oxford there they were, waiting for me. Now I don't even give them a second glance!

I had to be put on a food programme eliminating my allergens. I was prescribed a number of natural vitamins and minerals that almost filled my carrier bag but it was what happened next that really blessed both me and my husband. Pearl said as we were leaving that she felt led to pray with both of us.

She not only prayed over us both, breaking so many ancestral curses over us together as man and wife, but cast out many spirits in the name of Jesus: fear, rejection and a broken heart as well, plus many other spirits that were not of God's kingdom. Finally Pearl anointed us with oil on both head and feet. I fell in the Spirit, knowing that God had touched me and that He was going to heal me, praise His holy name!

Both my husband and I went home feeling blessed and we praised God all the way home, saying what a wonderful God we have. I have been to the Clinic now for five months in which time I have felt so much better I find that I have much more energy than before. My housework does not seem to be the mountainous task that it was before and it has been a gradual goodbye to my cough.

God has given me a new life. All my allergies have gone, praise His wonderful name. God is so good for I have been set free. I have also learned with Daniel that sometimes we have to fast every pleasant thing! My workmates have noticed a difference in me. My daughters too were delighted to see me look so well and happy, as the improvement in me was evident as the weeks went by, and my dear husband says that he has a new wife.'

At the time Tony and Doreen came to me I had no idea, one doesn't, of what preceeded their arrival. I was very amused when I heard. I will let Tony explain:

'Doreen's cough was driving me nuts and we planned to get away from it all, in case it was just her nerves shredded after so much sorrow. I always enjoy a holiday, planning the next excursion, but to my annoyance Doreen was glued to Pearl's book.

"Listen to this, Tony, just listen to this."

On and on it went. To keep the peace I would stop my map reading and go into the caravan whilst Doreen gave me yet more chapter and verse. I knew that we were looking in faith for a cure for my dear wife. Her whole life had been chequered with hurts and disappointments, leaving her self-protective and full of defence at the slightest suggestion of criticism.

My mind was not really on the words coming from her excited mouth. Who was this Pearl Coleman anyway? What on earth were all these spirits she kept referring to? After reading a whole chapter she began coughing again, that unholy curse that was destroying my dear Doreen, that cough that stopped us from entertaining our friends and even our dear grandchildren that we loved so much, that curse that I had no answer for. I had had six and a half years of it. I was fed up.

"Read the next chapter, Darling," she croaked between bouts of coughing. Full of sadness I took the book, secretly pressing the Lord in my mind with that well worn question,

"Why do you not heal my darling wife?"

As I began to read the book to her my mind was now engaged in much concentration and very slowly the stories of those that had been healed began to register in my mind. Who was this woman Pearl Coleman? Could all these things that had been happening to others help Doreen?

It was now very late and Doreen became as usual ready for bed hours before I was ready to sleep. I kissed this creature so full of disappointment and hurt goodnight, feeling so desperate and inadequate to help her with all her many ailments. As I began to tidy up the awning and set up my bed my mind reflected the wisdom of risking another disappointment. Time after time we had tried to find a way of healing my Darling.

I could not sleep. It was far too early for me to sleep anyway, but my heart yet again went out to the Lord for my wife. I have always been taught to speak to the Lord with great respect but enough was enough. I was angry and spoke with bluntness and without respect.

"Lord, we have done everything we can think of! Trip after trip to the hospital, visit after visit to the doctors."

I listed all the many contraptions and medicines that filled the entire top drawer of our bedside cabinet and the many bottles of Codeine Linctus that seemed to be the only drug that could soften that cough.

Many a double visit to the chemist was made in attempts to obtain this drug, now so difficult to get as a result of the many drug addicts using it to get on a cheap high. How we hated having to sign our name after each purchase. One of us would make a purchase first, then after a short while the other would go in and ask for more. This was the only way we could amass enough stock of the linctus which alone seemed to work. It made us feel guilty but was the only drug that gave relief to that curse.

I reflected on all the many prayers so many of our dear friends had offered for my dear Doreen and how our dear Pastor, a man full of deep love and empathy, encouraged the whole Church to pray against this cough. The prayers were often answered for a short while but as soon as the prayers gave way to other pressing matters the cough would return once more, gripping my darling wife, and all I could do was watch her suffer helplessly in the background.

"Lord, why do you not answer all these prayers? Why do you not hear my cries. Why can't we claim the victory?"

I complained to the Lord with much anger of all the sleepless nights being awoken by the loud coughing and the violent movements in the bed as she coughed and coughed, crying out to the Lord in tears of desperation. I knew that the time was coming that I soon would not be able to cope any longer with this destroyer of our happiness and for my own health I would need peace. I thought of divorce. Almost as a slight against my prayers Doreen started ten minute rounds of coughing as soon as I said the word "Amen".

The following morning I awoke early to find the sun pouring through a slit in the curtains onto the floor where the book was left. I began to read more of the ministry of this woman Pearl Coleman but with some reserve.

Later that day I completely broke down out of sheer frustration after many small attacks of coughing throughout the day. Doreen had a very bad attack in the car and was sick everywhere. I could not stand it any longer. This was supposed to be a restful time, but we were not even given one day's rest from this persistent, aggravating cough. I stopped the car in the middle of this beautiful country lane and slammed the door in anger as I shouted to the Lord,

"I have not got the strength to live with this woman any longer."

I could see Doreen weeping in the car. I knew that I had hurt her terribly but I could not stand this cough that shook me every time it came like a loud cymbal, crashing from nowhere, destroying the peace and harmony of this lovely woman. No longer could I stand all the weakness and irritation that was the ruin of our holiday, our social life and our marriage.

But it was not her fault and I really did love her. She was the woman that God had chosen for me after much prayer. Soon I felt ashamed as I looked back at her unhappy face in the car. What sort of a Christian was I supposed to be, a lay preacher for many years, a youth leader of a very successful Christian youth club, a man whom God had really blessed and had pulled through so many hard times. Why was I acting in this way to someone that I had grown to love so much?

I went back to the car feeling like the world's greatest living Christian fraud, a little calmer. Now slowly I began to explain to this poor, hurt woman that I really did love her, and how I felt so frustrated over all of her sickness and her cough that tested our faith in God's healing power. As each day of our holiday passed we read more and more of the work of Pearl Coleman and decided to contact her as soon as we got back home.

As I returned back to the humdrum of the electrical industry, time for further reading of Pearl's book was stolen as the long hours demanded of industry in fighting recession took their toll of my leisure time. But Doreen wrote and made an appointment to see Pearl at her Clinic at Woking. Little did I realize that this was to be a turning point in our marriage and my understanding of the battle that is at this time raging throughout the earth. Spiritual warfare!

Something was happening to me that seemed to be putting stumbling blocks in my way as if to stop me from taking Doreen to Pearl's Clinic. How was I to get time off work? Where was the money coming from? Was this going to be another big disappointment? Do all these spirits that Pearl writes about really exist? Well, I'd go and look her over. After working as a research technologist for many years my mind works only by investigation and experience, not by the word of others. I just had to investigate this woman's ministry.

I asked the Lord to clear the way for us. Everything bit by bit fell into place. I was given time off work. Doreen came into a small legacy. But as we travelled along the motorway my thoughts were of how to console my wife if all failed! "Lane End" was found after little trouble and the whole place reflected a presence I have felt many times when I have been close to God. There was no doubt the Clinic was special.

We both prayed before we walked to the main door and rapped the knocker. Doreen was interviewed by Henrietta and Ruth took down not only the usual medical information but all of Doreen's hurts and disappointments as well, This was different! My first impression of Pearl was a bit of a shock as she spoke with the authority that reminded me of a ward sister. We were ushered upstairs into a consulting room where a large number of tests were carried out to establish if Doreen had Candidosis.

The interview was interrupted for a little and I felt strongly to pray for Pearl. I did so out loud. I thought that I had embarrassed her but instead she thanked me. I felt a deep love in her and a strength that was God given, a very special strength. After a great many tests Doreen was told that she was a very bad case of Candidosis and Pearl was amazed that Doreen was still able to walk about, let alone going out to work three days a week! Now I knew it could only have been prayers that had kept my Doreen going until now.

She finished up with a new type of diet and a great many natural vitamins and minerals that Pearl had prescribed for her. But what came next was both beautiful and moving. Pearl prayed over us with members of her staff.

After a freedom from curse prayer over us Pearl began to cast out spirits in both of us. I actually felt a cleansing going on in my body. Doreen fell in the Spirit on to the floor and Pearl anointed Doreen, then myself, on the head and feet with oil, cutting us off from witchcraft at the feet. We went home blessed and cleansed of all our earthly and spiritual burdens. We felt wonderfully uplifted and we praised God at 60 mph on the M40! A great joy filled the car all the way home.

The next morning my feet still tingled and at my place of work there are many stairs that would tire me out, but today I flew up them like a young athlete. As the days went by Doreen became very depressed due to the cleansing out of her body from all the drugs and foods that brought about her many allergies. Pearl had pointed out that there might be withdrawal symptoms, just as with heroin, and that the worse they were, the more toxins were clearing out. Again I was having to support her but she persevered with her diet and slowly after the first week she began to gather a new strength.

As the weeks passed Doreen was transformed into a young fawn that sang in her kitchen, going about her wifely duties as if she were many years younger. I lost well over a stone in weight by eating the same food as her, and was amazed I could eat so much and lose weight. We have become more and more aware of our need to be in constant tune with this ministry that Pearl carries and the change in both of us has been commented on by our Church, family and friends.

As for Doreen's allergies, they have all gone! I have a new wife, younger and happier. She is more positive in her planning and her cough weakens by the week. I know that the Lord will completely heal my lovely Doreen. I will never forget what happened at the "Lane End" Clinic and Pearl has left me full of gratitude for allowing God to use her and her home in this way. To my astonishment that first ministry was not the last, but I will now hand you over to Pearl.'

On their second visit, in spite of the progress made, I sensed an undercurrent of impatience and criticism in this lovely couple. Doreen was constantly on the defensive when she was not being attacked. Tony was guilty of lording his superior engineer's brain and thought pattern over her. I felt he unwittingly talked down to her.

She was fed up with the money he spent on his cruiser and the time occupied by his model railway. I ultimately saw this, and indeed it was quite the most spectacular affair I have ever seen! I discerned it was an idol. Tony was a peach of a man but, like all collectors of the spectacular, he had pride in his achievement and indeed he had no mean brain!

I recall quite unexpectedly hustling Doreen into the sitting room after their consultation, leaving Henrietta with the next patient. Ruth joined us. I spoke to Doreen alone first, and such a mantle fell on me I could hardly believe my ears. I rebuked her in love for her constant self-defence and self-justification, and subsequently ministered to her, calling out a 'waif and stray' spirit, and the spirit of a skivvy. These were new ones to me!

Then Tony joined her on the sofa. I prayed the counsel of wisdom and might (Isaiah 11) over myself and began. It wasn't me. It was so tough, but I could feel the love of God in me pouring out for this marriage. I found myself speaking quite strongly to Tony concerning pride, idolatry and anger. Ruth was praying in the Spirit all the while. As the words poured out I expected this man to be offended and leave.

Later that night I got a call from Tony. He said these words, I wrote them down:

'Do you realise the anointing upon your life and your ministry, Pearl? Only the Holy Spirit could have told you so many things about me, because only He knew. What is more I never ever believed I could take all that from a woman, but I bless you because a great healing of our marriage has taken place and God has dealt with me. Can I tell you, Pearl, our marriage was under such stress?'

So the prophet in Kuala Lumpur had heard from God, and this is only one case of many that I am relating. Tony's words encouraged me to go on in this field. Tony and Doreen come socially to the Clinic and support the ministry team, but the Lord has told me that their home will be an oasis for those who have suffered deeply, praise His name!

Whilst roughing out this chapter I realised that Doreen always coughed just a little when at the Clinic or in my company. I addressed the Lord as I concluded this chapter with the words,

'What a pity we cannot say that Doreen is entirely free from her cough.'

We all felt that this last bit was spiritual, as though

taunting me that I hadn't quite got it! The reply from the Holy Spirit came in a flash. Two words:

'Codeine Linctus.'

Codeine is an opium derivative so it has to be called out, like all drug spirits. It was challenged and left in the name of Jesus and Doreen's cough departed completely. The final piece in the jigsaw! All the glory goes to Jesus, praise His wonderful name!

Just see what Jehovah Jireh did in His wonderful provision for this lovely couple, even getting their houses to back on to one another! Tony and Doreen are now counselling patients for me and joining us at the ministry teachings and fellowship at every opportunity. We all love having them join us, praise the Lord!

Chapter 20

The Plug-In Drug

We continue at the Clinic to ask our patients how many hours they watch television, as opposed to reading the Bible. I went into this in some detail in my last book, *The Anointing Breaks the Yoke*, chapter 10, 'Television and the Church'. I do not propose to repeat myself here but I do want to sound the alarm bell yet again.

Many Christians will say they want the television for the news. The news, good people, is in the Bible. Be certain that the news on television is exactly what the powers that be, satanic powers, want you to be programmed to absorb.

Tell me, do you see accurate reporting on events in Israel, for example? Or do you see news heavily slanted against God's people, and inviting us to believe in the not even remote possibility of peace without surrendered land? I could go on.

I had a most terrible dream last year. In my dream I was showing new patients photographs of the Clinic. When I showed the photograph of the sitting room, to my utter astonishment there was a golden image in the picture which was clearly an idol. It looked a bit like a totem pole with a bird-like head and spread wings on top. In my dream I recall remarking,

'That's peculiar, I thought I had removed everything occult from the sitting room years ago.'

Then I awoke. The dream troubled me and I sat in the sitting room contemplating it on many occasions. I got a strong witness in my spirit that there was an idol in the sitting room. I looked around. It could only be one thing, the television set.

I hardly ever used it. I loathe it, as most people know, because it destroys family life, corrupts viewers and is a time-wasting, seducing, mesmeric spirit. I was quite perplexed because the television had been, to my annoyance, constantly used by a guest.

I shared with a sister who had a husband who was a TV addict. She told me how one night, when the Lord convicted her that her husband was worshipping at this shrine every night, she got out of bed and knelt in the room where it was and repented of the shrine in her home on his behalf. She took authority over the addiction and other spirits emanating from this source, following which there was a decline in viewing and subsequent total lack of interest. I decided to do the same thing. I got on my knees and confessed the idolatry as though it had been my own and I exorcised the spirit of idolatry, with a marked effect. Thank you Jesus!

> 'And you hath he quickened, who were dead in trespasses and sins; Wherein in time past ye walked according to the course of this world, according to the prince of the power of the air; the spirit that now worketh in the children of disobedience: Among whom also we all had our conversation in times past in the lusts of our flesh and of the mind; and were by nature the children of wrath, even as others.'
>
> (Ephesians 2:1–3)

TV and radio operate through the realm controlled by the prince of the power of the air, the spirit that now works in the children – which includes adults – of disobedience, by means of the lusts of our flesh and our minds, bringing God's wrath. Please remember that!

Now I am not saying that sometimes there are not incredible documentaries or wildlife films on TV. But how rare, so rare is the person who will not keep it on for just one more programme and then select something which is promised on the screen for later on.

The box manipulates and controls lives, it fills peoples heads with the acceptability of pornography and violence. To my great joy Merlin Carothers, author of *Prison to Praise* and *Power of Praise*, has written a book about television entitled *Are You Sitting Comfortably?*

If there is a word in season it surely is this book. Published by Kingsway at £3.50, I defy any Christian television addicts to read it and not tremble in their boots. It is an awesome book on idolatry. It confirmed every discernment I wrote of concerning television.

I sat down and read it in one day and evening. I could quote piece after piece of wisdom and revelation from that awe-inspiring narrative on what the idolatry of television cost that lovely man, Merlin Carothers. He should be knighted by the Body of Christ for his services to the King, in his humbling confession that all men may read. God bless you abundantly, dear brother Merlin. Thank you for your obedience, your transparency and noble honesty. Here are a few quotations and comments from the book (and he uses the NIV except where stated):

Page 26

>'Even the comedies stretched as far as they could to make fun of morality.'

Page 27

'We have circled our favourites, programmed them onto our VCRs io avoid missing anything while we go to Church.'

'God's solid foundation stands firm, sealed with this inscription: The Lord knows those who are His, and, everyone who confesses the name of the Lord must turn away from wickedness.' (2 Timothy 2:19)

Page 29

'The more a person is addicted to a vice, the less he cares for advice!'

Page 30

'Too many of us have the perception that if we can just make it to heaven, that is more than enough.'

Page 35

'It's not funny to realise that we, who call ourselves servants of God have too often allowed ourselves to become servants of the 'machine' called television ... The television was my daily companion – an absorbing friend.'

Page 36

'Do not be misled. Bad company corrupts good character.' (1 Corinthians 15:33)

And then he pleads,

'Come back to your senses as you ought, and stop sinning.' (1 Corinthians 15:34)

In 2 Corinthians 6:14 I found another painful verse:

> *'Do not be yoked together with unbelievers. For what do righteousness and wickedness have in common? Or what fellowship can light have with darkness?'*

Page 43

> *'Get rid of all moral filth,'* God clearly commanded in James 1:21. And in verse 27, *'Keep yourself from being polluted by the world.'*

He goes on to warn:

> *'Escape the corruption in the world caused by evil desires.'* (2 Peter 1:4)

> *'For he that soweth to his flesh shall of the flesh reap corruption; but he that soweth to the Spirit shall of the Spirit reap life everlasting.'*
>
> (Galatians 6:8 KJV)

Page 60

> *'It is enough for the student to be like his teacher, He said, and the servant like his master.'*
>
> (Matthew 10:25)

He explained further,

> *'I have set you an example that you should do as I have done to you . . . '* (John 13:15)

2 Samuel 22:33 reminds us: *'It is God who arms me with strength . . . '*

> *'Do not fear, for I am with you; do not be dismayed, for I am your God. I will strengthen you and help you; I will uphold you with my righteous right hand.'*
>
> (Isaiah 41:10)

Page 65

> 'See to it, therefore, that you conduct yourselves carefully, not as foolish but as wise people who make the best possible use of their time, because these are evil days.' (Ephesians 5:15–16 ML)

Page 77

> 'Clothe yourselves with the Lord Jesus Christ; do not make provision for the flesh to gratify its cravings.' (Romans 13:14 ML)

> 'I know your deeds, that you are neither cold nor hot. I wish you were either one or the other! So, because you are lukewarm – neither hot nor cold – I am about to spit you out of my mouth.'
> (Revelation 3:15–16)

Well that's a few. The book contains at least a hundred references confirming our Father's abhorrence of this time-wasting, soul-destroying, relationships-destroying spirit.

I was at an African Christian party recently and the television got turned on at one end of a large room. I was quick to observe the mesmerism that followed and the sudden disinterest of the group so affected in the lovely things that were going on at the party to glorify the Lord. I was very cutting about it, but then I would be. To me to have the television on when such a gathering is taking place is really not on.

I think probably one of the children turned it on. But parents, please understand, you may be responsible for your childrens' idolatry and you do not have to have it on for the sake of peace!

Chapter 21

The Old Lady

I recall driving out to a favourite beauty spot quite late one winter's afternoon. The light was fading but there had been some lovely winter sunshine last thing, and a friend and I decided to take the air.

We were driving up a very steep hill on a narrow road when suddenly police were everywhere. I knew we could not possibly make it to where we planned to walk from, so we quickly turned round and edged off the road to a car park which accommodated cars for another popular walk. It was clay soil and since it had been raining hard all day it was not a walk I would have chosen.

However, by the time we parked we observed a complete road block formed by all manner of police vehicles. We had no idea what was going on but were pleased not to be held up on the steep hillside.

As we took the pathway down the steep bank we were slipping about all over the place. I was clinging to my friend's arm, the light was virtually non-existent between the hedgerows. Black clouds were scurrying overhead.

'There has been torrential rain here,' I remarked as I tentatively placed one foot before the other.

We arrived at the little lane at the foot of the hill. It was absolutely like a flowing stream and so muddy. Fortunately our walking boots were waterproof and we simply waded along the lane. Certainly there was no turning back because climbing up the slippery slope would be worse than the downward journey.

'There's a little turning off to the left up here, I don't think it will be so muddy,' I said as we trundled along.

After a short distance, and thanking God for our waterproof boots, we turned off left by some small farm cottages which appeared to be deserted. Suddenly we were confronted by the voice of a frail old lady, descending the steps to one of the cottages. She looked terrified in the rapidly fading light.

'Help me, please help me,' she entreated.

My friend was by her side in a flash. I was binding the spirit of fear manifesting in intensity in the dear soul as she clung eagerly to the arm extended to her. I looked at her frightened face, her soaking wet plimsolled feet and shredded stockings as I asked her,

'Did you fall?'

'Yes. I got so bored indoors I thought I would take a walk. I used to know the people in these cottages, but I'm eighty-three now. I forgot, you see. It only seems like yesterday, but I'm lost now. Could you tell me where I am?'

Supporting each arm, we were literally holding her up. Clearly our walk had to be postponed. I was staring at her soddened, plimsolled feet in disbelief when she told me she could only get that footwear on because of her toenails.

'I'm a bit deaf, dear,' she went on, 'Where am I?'

I asked her loudly where she lived and she said Albury. I could not believe it, she must have walked a good two miles. My friend said to me,

160

'Pearl, wherever she lives, we have to escort her right back.'

Well, we almost carried her back to her cottage. She was soaking wet. It was a neat little cottage and she wanted us to stay. We explained that she ought to get cleaned up and warm and dry and somehow we had to get back another way in the dark. We prayed with her before leaving.

What a laugh that was. We were about as muddy as she was when we met her, but we loved it. As we were walking the old lady back I said to her,

'Do you know Jesus?'

She replied,

'I most certainly do, my God is always with me.'

'That's just what we thought,' we replied laughingly, looking at each other.

Jehovah Jireh made us His provision for that dear soul. We never found out what the police were up to, but that did not matter. A lovely old lady would soon be safely tucked up in bed.

Chapter 22

Prayer for Stabbed Girl

In April 1994 I was walking with two friends across my favourite Surrey countryside. Hazel catkins were dancing, bluebells and red campion pushing up through the leaf-moulded forest floor. Lambs leapt for joy in just about every field, whilst lazy cattle chewed the cud on an unbelievably hot spring day.

We crossed fields with silver ribboned streams winding through them, their banks muddied by the visitation of thirsty cattle and horses. I could feel that urgency to get my legs going and was loving the solid feeling of good walking boots with which to cover the terrain.

It was a day of laughter and sharing under those incredibly blue skies. Dulcie and Ron had snatched some rare time from their boarding house for a day out. They always seem to bring the sunshine with them, even if it starts out wet!

We had enjoyed a super lunch at the Old Mill, Gomshall and were heading in a wide circular walk towards the Clock House Tea Rooms at Abingher Hammer for one of Angela's lovely watercress teas. The watercress is grown locally and is unbeatable for that lovely mustardy flavour and freshness.

Our conversation changed tenor suddenly as Dulcie relayed a most terrible story of a girl dying in intensive care in Dover, following a horrific attack by a rapist. She was apparently discovered under a hedge by a lorry driver, so beaten up that he thought she was a dead animal. She had many stab wounds and her jaw was broken.

We were all just climbing over a style when this conversation took place. I took a few steps into the field we were to cross, awaiting the other two to cross the style and follow. I had not gone very far when I found I could hardly walk straight. I also found myself bending over my own stomach.

An anointing rose up within me of such power I knew we had to pray. We stood together as words for mercy poured out of my mouth, lifting this battered girl up to the Almighty. I had literally no sense of being on a walk or in a field. I knew the intercession had been mightily laid on my heart by the Lord I served.

I cried out to God to raise her up miraculously, and that she would come to know the Lord Jesus and see her healing as a miraculous intervention of the Lord. The prayers continued flowing out of my mouth until the others said 'Amen'. We reminded the Lord of this prayer of agreement, and birthed what I had prayed by lifting her up while praying in the Spirit together. I then said,

'I believe our prayers have availed and that she is healed, that God heard.'

We continued our walk and the next thing I learned from Dulcie was that the injured girl was out of intensive care and out of hospital.

Dulcie sent me the press cuttings and I could see that it was a totally unexpected physical recovery.

The temptation to want to know more is always great.

Her name was never mentioned in the press, so I could not write to her. Really, I do not think God wanted me to, but just to trust that the Bible means what it says:

> '*The effectual fervent prayer of a righteous man availeth much.*'
>   (James 5:16b)

Unknown to that young woman she had a Jehovah Jireh who provided her with intercessors at a time of need. Praise His holy and merciful name!

Chapter 23

Ernest

There are very few people visiting the Clinic who do not ask about Ernest. Fortunately he is still with us on some Clinic days. When I wrote about Ernest in *Fruit Abiding in the Vine*, chapters 3 and 4, he was seventy-seven. He is now in his eighty-first year.

Readers will recall no doubt my dreadful accident which was followed by the medical mishap of my arm being set in plaster too tightly by the hospital, my becoming paralysed, and how this terrible injury and all that transpired was a demonic attack to polish me off for sure! Surgery to cut the nerves did not restore the circulation. I suffered death of nerves and muscles and the awful revelation that I had advanced brittle bone disease.

Ernest was tucked up comfortably in bed one night when Jehovah Jireh used him as an intercessor to pray for my life, as I was literally being suffocated in my own bed with my own duvet by satanic hands! I was in agony with so many broken bones from the accident and an overweight plaster of Paris on my arm. Black despair engulfed me as I struggled to free myself from Satan. Again, I will not repeat the whole episode here but I finally overcame the enemy, although I was totally exhausted, sleep having evaded me for weeks anyway.

However, I am going to repeat a little from pages 15–16 of the chapter entitled 'Revelation'. I am going to do this because the Lord has prompted me in this whole book to be reminded of His grace, mercy and provision. I need to be reminded as the enemy seeks right now to tear down the Clinic and the Ministry by attacking me with probably the worst vengeance I have experienced from him, and that is saying something!

Ernest came the following morning to tell me about what happened to him so unexpectedly the night before as I struggled with Satan:

'The moment Ernest entered the bedroom I could detect that he was different. His face was as red and glowing as a sunset. He was clutching his Bible and a piece of paper.

"What is it Ernest?" I enquired.

"Last night I went to bed as usual at about ten o'clock. I said my prayers and fell asleep. As you know I usually sleep like a top, but at about one o'clock in the morning I was awakened by myself praying in a very loud and strange tongue. It was so fast and strong, it was not my usual tongue. The Lord told me to get up and pray. I slid out of bed, my mouth was so dry, my tongue ached, it was moving so fast. I made sure to look at the clock.

"I prayed for about an hour when suddenly I was transported in the Spirit to the Clinic. I found myself with my back against the consulting room window looking out at the garden. I could clearly see the bird bath, the bird table and the boundary hedge. My feet were astride the whole grounds. I felt as if each one was placed on a spiritual wall."

By this time tears were streaming down Ernest's face, and he took the piece of paper he had placed on his Bible. He had to calm himself.

"A voice, I know it was the Lord, spoke to me so clearly. It was not faint and it was a command. I wrote it down as soon as I could, I felt it was so important."

He read out from the piece of paper,

"Stand astride the city of God which is my daughter's house and ward off the powers of darkness."

He continued, "I found myself with my legs astride this spiritual wall, pushing out against a mighty force. During the second hour of praying in the Spirit I thought I should telephone someone. I considered this several times but was commanded to pray on.

"The danger seemed to subside and I was kept praying at intervals until 4.00 am, then at lesser intervals until about 6.00 am when I was exhausted.

"Later in the morning when I read what I had written there was a space and I had written two words, 'The devil'. I believe that was after I had such a desire to ring someone, and stop praying in the Spirit. My tongue was dry."

I was able to check out the times with my own dreadful experience that night, and clearly it was a battle against the powers of darkness.'

The Clinic now incorporates City of God Ministries, on which word brought by Ernest it was formed. Ernest was Jehovah Jireh's provision for me from the time of my injury in 1988 until January 1993. He fed me, ferried me from hospital to fracture clinics, to physios, to doctors galore. If he could not drive me long distance to specialists in London, he hired a car to transport me. He watered my garden, planted out my bedding plants, fetched and carried all manner of shopping, went to the bank for me and attended to my every need.

At this time in my life when I felt so ugly, not even being able to put my arm through sleeves, he made me feel treasured. I might add that I was, being a hard worker always, bad tempered, frustrated, irritable through never-ending nerve pain and generally disappointed with the Lord for allowing such an accident, until I had the revelation that I had cursed the arms He had made. Again, that is all in the book and when I look back I can hardly believe the way the Lord healed me, but He did.

Here was a man of God with the patience of Job. And he needed it! I planned a secret eightieth tea party at the Clinic for Ernest, and dinner party afterwards at a local restaurant which looks after our celebrations. He had a lovely open Bible cake with personal Scriptures on, decorated with doves.

All the old team and the newer members travelled from far and wide to celebrate Ernest's eightieth birthday. He was quite overcome by gifts and messages of love. We do all love him so much. Rufus paid tribute to Ernest's never-ending hospitality, and I wrote him the following poem as a token of my deep love in Jesus and my heartfelt thanks to him as a special brother in Christ.

He still looks only about sixty, but he needs prayer for his knees. We are praying the Lord will regenerate them because Ernest still has so much to offer us all. Join me in these prayers, please.

Ernest is 80 Today

Our dear Ernest is eighty today,
And there's so much that I wanted to say,
For when he was only seventy three

He said 'Pearl, the Lord has spoken to me.
He told me quite plainly to look after you
And that is what I am going to do.'

I was so wounded, in pain and in bed,
But I looked in his eyes and I heard what he said.
My mind was engulfed with the blackest despair
But I witnessed in Ernest such love and such care.
And I knew that my brother meant every word,
And most surely from Father in heaven had
     heard.

I was listless and lifeless, in horrible pain,
But dear Ernest was there in the sun and the rain.
He drove me on journeys both near and so far,
Becoming a chauffeur in his lovely car.
To fracture clinics, hospitals, doctors galore,
To X-ray units and very much more.
He ferried me food and he combed out my hair,
And when I was wretched he always was there.

And in this dear man's unconditional love
I saw our dear Saviour from heaven above.
Then one day he rang me, I looked such a fright:
My body unwashed, my hair tangled, a sight.
For I'd wrestled with Satan all through the night
And black was my outlook and gone was the light.

I told him 'You can't come, I am such a mess.'
Imagine what happened, I'm sure you can guess.
For he was insistent, and came in a rush
His eyes full of tears and his face all a-flush.
On the night that I'd fought for my life in my bed
The Lord had come to dear Ernest and said:

**'Stand astride the city of God, which is my
     daughter's house.'**

He awoke from his slumber and pinned back his
    ears,
He leapt out of bed and he stifled his fears.
It was a command, in his ear loudly rung,
And he found himself using a different tongue.
On and on for hours he went,
His mouth became dry, his energy spent.

He wanted to pause for a breather, or flop,
But he knew in his heart that he dared not stop.
To the Clinic transported in spirit he found,
His back to the window high above ground.
His feet either side on a spiritual wall,
He extended his hands and pushed back with his
    all.
'Push back the powers of darkness' he heard,
And he knew without doubt that it came from the
    Lord.

And I watched his countenance as he spoke,
And I knew for certain it wasn't a joke.
That as I'd lain struggling and choking in bed,
With my duvet wrapped tightly around my head,
That the Lord had used this most precious friend
To stand with me firmly against the fiend.

There are many other things I could tell,
And it's easy to smile and to laugh when you're
    well,
But I wish you to know, and I'm sure you all do,
That Ernest has given me friendship so true.
For he placed his dear hands on my head when I
    wept,
And prayed over me as I fitfully slept.

He never shouted at me or railed,
Throughout each crisis his love prevailed.

Through every pain and every strife,
I could trust brother Ernest with my life.
So raise your glasses with great joy today,
Dear Ernest, we wish you 'Happy Birthday'.
May you have joy on the path you now tread,
And our dear Lord bless every hair on your head.

Thank you, Lord, for such wonderful provision of a man who esteemed me in Christ Jesus, tolerated all my faults and made allowances for my pain. Bless him, Lord, Amen.

Chapter 24

Obedience

We have to understand the Word of God or we cannot have any conception of what obedience is. There is a particular qualification for holy obedience, and it is the ability to trust God whatever.

You may be in a terrible wilderness and crying out to see fruit in your life. Please remember you do not bear fruit in the wilderness. It is a place that is barren and dry. What is important in the wilderness is what you are allowing God to do to you!

You may have indeed borne much fruit, but the Lord may want to reveal his secrets to you and prune you back some more. Remember John 15:1–2:

> *'I am the true vine, and My Father is the husband-man. Every branch in Me that beareth not fruit He taketh away: and every branch that beareth fruit, He purgeth it, that it may bring forth more fruit.'*

Make a study of all John 15, and another key word is 'abiding' in John 15:5–7. Apart from Him we can do nothing and apart from Him we have to be in the flesh. When I really listen to Him, not infrequently I have to do the very opposite of what I think would be right and proper.

Jesus said,

> *'If ye love Me, keep my commandments ... If a man love Me, He will keep My words.'*   (John 14:15, 23a)

Obeying God's commandment is the bedrock, the absolute foundation of walking in holiness. The Bible does not say if ye love Me you will go to the Church on Sunday. It speaks of keeping His commandments. How can we obey if we do not know what they are?

In John 13:34 Jesus speaks of a new commandment:

> *'A new commandment I give unto you. That ye love one another: as I have loved you, that ye also love one another.'*

How many of us do that really? Do we really love? I do not think we do. Of course there are exceptions but this love is not conditional on liking someone or them being nice to you. There are so many Scriptures to encourage us to love, but if indeed the Church were ever mindful of this love, would there be so much strife and division?

There are two kingdoms, one of light, one of darkness. The kingdom of darkness is the kingdom of this world and Satan is the Prince of this world. In John 18:36:

> *'Jesus answered, My kingdom is not of this world: if My kingdom were of this world, then would My servants fight, that I should not be delivered to the Jews: but now is My kingdom not from hence.'*

Members of the kingdom of darkness organise themselves without any reference to the Scriptures. Would you say the Church may be a little guilty of this?

Obedience is the requirement for divine blessing. It is the essential for seeing Jehovah Jireh operating in your life. Disobedience nullifies our right to expect assistance and deliverance from all evil.

Obedience also requires that we use the authority that the Word of God says we have, Luke 10:19. How many serpents and scorpions are you treading on? Do you recognise one when you see it? Ouch! If we obey those in the kingdom of darkness we shall be subject to the fruit of it, Romans 6:16. The Scriptures are full of references to men and women, even those of God, who obeyed Satan to their cost.

The blessings for obedience are, as I said in *Fruit Abiding in the Vine*, in Deuteronomy 28. I do not propose to list them here, but look at Exodus 15:26:

> *'If thou will diligently hearken to the voice of the Lord thy God, and wilt do that which is right in His sight, and wilt give ear to His commandments, and keep all His statutes, I will put none of these diseases upon thee, which I have brought upon the Egyptians: for I am the Lord that healeth thee.'*

This is not a demand for you to be perfect. You are **being** perfected. So am I, and I think God finds He has a hard job on His hands sometimes, but I know that is when I do not stop and listen.

My secretary Ruth drives me nuts sometimes. When I ask what she thinks she invariably says 'Have you asked Him?' We do ultimately get around to how she feels or her opinion, which she frequently points out may not that of the Lord! So often she is right and when I've checked it out with the Lord, invariably I barely need to know hers and we always end up laughing.

We have indeed to learn obedience and usually it is the hard way, from our mistakes, alas. 1 John 2:6 makes so clear that love and obedience are inseparable twins:

> *'He that saith he abideth in Him ought himself also so to walk, even as He walked.'*

Anyone knowingly disobedient, in rebellion against God's Word, is as easy to rescue as a man who has already drowned! Yes, indeed, we have God's mercy, and I continually cry out for it. (See my chapter on mercy in *The Anointing Breaks The Yoke*.)

When we first believed we read in the Word *'Repent and be baptised'* (Acts 2:38). Now if you have not been baptised, i.e. by personal commitment and full immersion, not infant sprinkling, you are in total disobedience. Whatever the circumstances, however inconvenient, do it now, in your bath if need be.

We baptise people in Ernest's bath if we cannot do it elsewhere. I actually feel that there is a little worldly ceremony becoming attached to baptism by immersion. I'm just slightly unhappy about it. I am not judging those who get involved with it, please note.

If you are waiting to be dipped with your friend you could be being disobedient. Where does Scripture say be baptised with your wife or husband or child or friend? Yes, it is nice if that conveniently happens, but *'Repent and be baptised'* is a command. It means **now**. The Bible does not say you have to do a study course first, either. That is **not** biblical.

Don't tell me new Christians have to have it explained to them. If they obey, the Holy Spirit will inform them as they come out of the water what it's all about! It is a simple obedience and ask questions afterwards! Derek Prince says when he leads people to the Lord, the next thing is to get them straight into the car and down to the river.

I had quite a bit of persecution from the church over my baptism, I can tell you. I had to live in a certain radius of miles from where the church with the baptistry was. Then I couldn't be baptised because I had a close friend who was a masonic doctor. Praise God, I did not know about the occultism of freemasonry then. I thought it was a little boys club! The moment Dr Joy Seevaratnam, also a former freemason, dipped me in the sea at Penang, a glorious memory, a few scales came off my eyes. I was able to witness to my friend and he renounced freemasonry.

Obedience to the Word of God decides your destiny, friends.

> *'Blessed are they that do His commandments, that they may have right to the tree of life, and may enter in through the gates into the city.'*
> (Revelation 22:14)

> *'For as by one man's disobedience many were made sinners, so by the obedience of One shall many be made righteous.'* (Romans 5:19)

> *'And being found in fashion as a man, He humbled himself, and became obedient unto death, even the death of the cross.'* (Philippians 2:8)

> *'Though He were a Son, yet learned He obedience by the things which He suffered; And being made perfect, He became the author of eternal salvation unto all them that obey Him.'* (Hebrews 5:8–9)

God said to Isaac he would perform the oath which he swore unto Abraham because *'Abraham obeyed my voice'* (Genesis 26:3–5). When we read in Genesis 22 the account of Abraham being ready to obey God, even to sacrificing his precious son Isaac, it should cause us to search our hearts to see what we are required in obedience to place on the altar! Personally, I get quite nervous of what the next thing will be! However, I trust God, so when I sense the next fire is due I check on my obedience and usually get a few shocks!

So many blessings are missed through disobedience. Things we could have almost overnight take years of attainment. Obedience is costly in terms of self, but disobedience is more costly. I implore you, obey and see Jehovah Jireh in your life.

A life yielded to self will be evidenced by lack of something, be sure of that! Psalm 23 says the Lord is our shepherd, therefore we shall lack nothing. I believe the small print is, if we obey.

In Acts the words of Peter tell us that God has given His Holy Spirit to them that obey Him. What Born Again believer does not want a constant revelation of the Holy Spirit at work in their lives?

If we are looking for true holiness as the Church, and obedience is the starting point of holiness, then we need to understand what Peter meant in 1 Peter 1:22:

> *'Seeing ye have purified your souls in obeying the truth through the Spirit unto unfeigned love of the brethren, see that ye love one another with a pure heart fervently.'*

Here again, do you see the link of the love and obedience? We cannot change what the Word of God tells us:

'But the word of the Lord endureth for ever. And this is the word which by the gospel is preached unto you.'
(1 Peter 1:25)

John made some frightening statements like telling us that if we say we know God and do not keep his commandments, then we are liars. **Liars**. Imagine that! Who is the father of all lies? Satan.

Disobedience brings separation from God. It's like being in a desert and thirsty. Jonah was driven from God's presence because he disobeyed. Jonah did splendid work as long as everything went smoothly, but the moment things were against him he went to pieces. If you crack up under stress, look for disobedience. There are always exceptions, I know, but even overwork to the point where stress, which can be healthy and stretching, becomes distress and the homoeostasis is undermined, can be disobedience.

Character is more than work. It is going through tests and trials, counting it all joy, and not cracking up under stress. When you are squeezed, what's in you comes out. Please let it be the Word of God!

God cannot really use anyone until they have the grace to forget themselves **entirely** and concentrate on Him. Have you seen folks at conferences looking at their watches as lunch time approaches? Or even rushing in for the evening session with bags of food? What we miss by breaking for lunch!

Obedience is definitely the pathway to spiritual power. We see so clearly in the life of our Lord obedience unto death as a man. His temptation in the wilderness, His daily battle with leaders in Jerusalem, the agony of Gethsemane and the terror of Calvary. During all those experiences His obedience was keen, intelligent and full.

Oh, how I pray I will never be so tested, but perilous

181

times are ahead and we should start now to practice obedience in small ways, like picking up the Bible in our spare time instead of grabbing a coffee and half an hour's television.

I want to tell you something. It is very simple. the more you obey God's Word the easier it becomes.

Our Father is a loving heavenly Father and He give us so many chances to come to heel, but like any earthly Father He is sometimes quite able and willing to shut us up in our room until we do as we are told!

I recall being shut in my room for disobedince. Usually it got so boring in there that I behaved myself in order to be let out. If you feel shut out from God and that nothing is going for you, try a week, that is seven days, of total obedience to His Word and watch Him move in Your life.

I know not a few mighty men and women who seem to have a stumbling block in their lives. That stumbling block, that hold-up or stagnation is usually just a small area in which they are unable to obey God. It does not matter how small it is, a little leaven leavens the whole lump, and the Father may be waiting for you to be faithful in a small way of obedience so He can fulfil all His promises in your life.

Very, very few of my patients do not recover completely and they arrive always having been under so many hospitals and doctors and therapists for treatment. I love it because I get the desperate and the desperate are always obedient.

'I'll do anything to get well' is always music to my ears.

Patients who do not recover are those who cannot do exactly what I ask. The difference between me and where they have had previous treatment is usually that they do not have to obey the practitioner. If people seek my help for debilitating sickness then I expect them to obey what I advise them is the cure. Likewise, our Father, having given us remedies for all our ills in His handbook, expects us to obey and recover.

I've just had to take my own medicine again. I have been neglecting what I know are basic disciplines for maintaining high energy levels and sparkle. I cannot plead ignorance, I know the rules! Two weeks towing the line transformed me mentally, physically and spiritually. I thought how stupid I was not to have realised the need for a refresher course sooner.

Do you need a refresher course on the Word of God? If you do, you need to study the Word daily, not when you feel like it!

If you find this, or any other form of obedience, difficult to do in your own strength, the Good News is that if you sincerely seek the Lord's help, asking Him to do it for you, you can trust Jehovah Jireh to bring it about in your life!

'For it is God which worketh in you both to will and to do of His good pleasure.' (Philippians 2:13)

Chapter 25

Finale

Ruth's Testimony

Jehovah Jireh provided Pearl and her Clinic for me after more than ten years virtually in bed with severe allergies, and also with what I discovered through her ministry to be demonic oppression, as is scripturally described in the Gospels.

I had been to countless churches, church groups, healing meetings and ministries during those years, desperately seeking relief. I do praise the Lord that I had been saved and born-again through one group, and in another He had unexpectedly healed my backache by giving me another half-inch in one leg! But the debilitating allergy continued, making it very difficult to manage even the simplest things.

I finally realised I would just have to wait on the Lord till He showed me what to do or where to go, putting myself entirely in His hands in the meantime. This really did take some trusting! He literally had to do everything for me, from getting me up in the morning to doing all the housework, shopping and cooking, even managing my conversations and relationships with people, and helping me sleep at night!

Finally in the autumn of 1992 I came across a copy of *Go and Do Likewise* on a friend's coffee table. My problems seemed nothing compared to what Pearl had been through and if she had found the answers, there was hope for me! One of Pearl's comments in her books was:

'You only do what you're desperate enough to do.'

I think the Lord may have let me wait such a long time so I would be desperate enough to do all I would need to, both physically and spiritually!

At last I did indeed receive the first truly effective and, for me, unheard of and wonderful, advice on how to get rid of such disabling allergies simply through the right diet and a few vitamin and mineral supplements. Even more liberating and providential, however, was the unique combination of Pearl's Ministry with her health Clinic.

A series of totally unexpected deliverances revealed a centuries-long Roman Catholic inheritance of religious persecution and oppression, dating back to the Reformation, and even to the satanic worship of Babylon, where many of the non-scriptural Catholic beliefs and practices are found, detail by detail! This was interspersed with the physical treatment I received over the following months, and eventually I felt so free I even offered to help out with the load of Clinic paperwork, in sheer gratitude for my first real chance of a healthy, happy and productive life, body, soul and spirit!

The scale of the healing and deliverance the Lord was ministering through Pearl, one of His most devoted servants, to countless people, both physically and spiritually, soon became evident. So did the most intense spiritual warfare to confuse and stop it! Only Jehovah Jireh could have provided the truly miraculous guidance and strength I needed to help with His work in her Clinic, this book and her next one *Refined By Fire*.

Just one of the reasons for such attack, no doubt, has been the Lord's provision of progressive healing and deliverance for me through both the Clinic work and books. His continuing revelation through Pearl's insights and experience, all the background information and the testimonies of others brings new areas needing confession, repentance and often self-deliverance, both for my own attitudes and actions and those of my ancestors. Praise the Lord, He is never finished with us, but we can confidently and joyfully trust Him to bring to completion all that He has begun in us!

Comment by Pearl

When Ruth came to the Clinic she was so spaced out and confused many would have thought her out of her mind! To be honest, I found her very draining and exhausting to be with. When The Lord told me to come alongside her out of Clinic hours I gasped,

'Give me something easy, Lord.'

But I obeyed. It wasn't really difficult because I sensed in this sister somebody really beautiful longing to be birthed, apart from the fact she had a very sharp brain which was being stunted by demonic oppression.

The rewards I have had for coming alongside Ruth have been so great, so treasured, so joyful. What is more I can see clearly that Jehovah Jireh was at work providing me with the best manuscript typist to date as she can actually read my writing, which often I can hardly do myself.

The Pastor of a church where I ministered recently in Penang prophesied some awesome things over me, including that I was 'on Satan's hit list, in the top five!'

'Satan hates you, Sister,' I was told.

Well, I can believe that. He certainly pays me a lot of attention so I guess I'm getting on his nerves. It is very tough sometimes, but I would rather be doing that than compromising with him.

Anyway, his fate is clearly recorded in the book of Revelation and I continually remind him of this. He knows as well as I do that it is one minute to midnight, so he is extra busy throughout the world at this time.

Praise God, we have the victory through the death of our precious Saviour, the Lord Jesus Christ.

Come quickly, Lord Jesus!

An Appeal

If I could make an appeal to the Body of Christ now, it would be for each reader to value the actual cost of writing a book or producing a teaching cassette or video. I am shocked when people tell me they are ninth on the list to borrow a book of mine! Ministries like ours are very dependent on book sales. Our lives in both the Clinic and Ministry would be transformed if every person who had read my books had bought and not borrowed them!

Likewise, if the books really blessed you, how about returning a copy to the publisher, to sow into our overseas mission and ministry in the third world? They will pass them on.

I used not to understand the copyright on cassette tapes, until I realised that those from my own library were being worn out by being copied without permission!

I give hundreds of my books away, as the Lord directs me. Sometimes I am astonished at how great the total is, but that is what ministry is all about.

Nevertheless, many Christian Book Shops are in real danger of disappearing if thay are not supported by actual purchases of publications. Readers need to know how hard it is to sustain a Christian presence in the High Street. Remember that when you are buying ministry books you are sowing into the ministry, and as you sow you shall reap! (2 Corinthians 9:6; Galatians 6:7–8).

If I can help you, please send a large A4 stamped addressed envelope. I will be happy to send you the Clinic papers. I can no longer reply to letters of ten pages (the average received) or give consultations by post.

Bless you for understanding how important it is for me to use my time wisely, and to guard against anything that can be used to keep me out of the Word!

Pearl Coleman